Home Winemaking
Techniques and Recipes

Home Winemaking Techniques and Recipes

RODNEY BOOTHROYD

ALLISON & BUSBY
LONDON / NEW YORK

Home Winemaking Techniques and Recipes
first published in Great Britain in 1985 by
Allison and Busby Limited
6a Noel Street, London W1V 3RB,
and distributed in the USA by
Schocken Books Inc.,
62 Cooper Square, New York, NY 10003.

British Library Cataloguing in Publication Data:

Boothroyd, Rodney
    Home winemaking: techniques and recipes.
    1. Wine and wine making
    I. Title
    641.8'72   TP548
    ISBN 0–85031–622–7

Set in 10/12 Sabon by Falcon Graphic Art, Wallington, Surrey
Printed and bound in Great Britain by
Richard Clay (The Chaucer Press) Ltd
Bungay, Suffolk

Contents

Acknowledgements

The author gratefully acknowledges advice and information
provided by:

Continental Wine Experts Limited
The Winery
Cawston
Norwich NR10 4BQ

Mr Neville Instone
Managing Director
Southern Vinyards Limited
Nizells Avenue
Hove
East Sussex BN3 1PS

Hoole Packing and Chemical Company Limited
26 Charles Street
Hoole
Chester CH2 3HF

(suppliers of *Contessa* brand wine concentrates)

The Boots Company PLC
Nottingham
NG2 3AA

Winemaker and Brewer Magazine
Argus Specialist Publications Limited
P O Box 35
Wolsey House
Hemel Hempstead
HP2 4SS.

And all the contributors of wine recipes.

List of illustrations

List of tables

If on my theme I rightly think,
There are five reasons why men drink:
Good wine, a friend, or being dry
(Or lest we should be by and by) —
Or any other reason why.

HENRY ALDRICH, 1648–1710

Introduction

You may have read or heard that the word "wine" should only be used to describe the fermented juice of the grape. Yet many home winemakers produce wines which rival the commercial product from fruits, flowers and vegetables. However, the high quality of home-made wines is not the only reason for the astonishing growth of this hobby in recent years. The fact that wine has become more widely known and accepted as an everyday drink is no doubt partly responsible for this rate of growth; so too is the remarkable difference in price between home-made and commercial wine — you can make six bottles of wine at home for the price of one bottle from the wine store. But perhaps the most important reason for the increase in popularity of home winemaking is the satisfaction involved in the creation of a truly enjoyable and useful finished product through one's own efforts.

Home-made wines are often called "country wines", presumably because the ingredients were originally obtained from the plants and trees of the countryside. But although the natural "harvests" of elderberries, blackberries, rosehips, sloes and so on remain staple ingredients of home-made wine, many other cultivated fruits now feature in the winemaker's recipe book. And, surprising as it may seem, wines of excellent quality can also be made from ordinary root vegetables, cereals and flower petals — the most famous of the latter undoubtedly being elderflower wine.

Even if you live in the middle of a town or city, winemaking with "country" ingredients is quite possible. There are many home winemaking shops which supply both dried and canned ingredients, as well as equipment and free advice. For those who wish to make their winemaking as simple as possible, there are now many high-quality grape-juice concentrates on the market. These can be made into wine in their own right, or they can be blended with other fruit and vegetables to add a certain extra character to the finished wine.

11

All in all, therefore, home winemaking is a fascinating, creative and enjoyable hobby — and one which has very few limits. If you start by making a single batch of red or white wine, before long you will undoubtedly find yourself making wine in large quantities, or trying to emulate commercial wines, or exhibiting your wine at local or national shows, or joining a "wine circle" to meet fellow winemakers and make new friends in your area.

In this book, I explain the basic procedures for making red and white wines from fruit, flowers, cereals and vegetables. There are 120 new recipes, as well as sections on specialized topics such as making sherry and sparkling wines. The whole book, although comprehensive, is written in a clear and concise style so that both the novice and the experienced winemaker should find it useful.

So wait no longer! If you are wondering how to start, take this book home, select a recipe, obtain the basic equipment and begin! Soon you will be enjoying your first glass of delicious home-made wine. (Do not be tempted, however, to take advantage of the ease and economy of making wine at home by selling the finished product. You may make as much wine as you like, but technically it is for your own consumption; to sell it would be illegal.)

PART 1

Winemaking at Home

The basis of winemaking

The fundamental stages involved in the making of any wine can be listed very simply. They are:

- extracting the flavour from the ingredients
- fermentation
- maturation and bottling

I shall explain these stages in detail later on, but an outline of the processes involved will be useful in understanding the equipment required for winemaking and the different ingredients and additives which go into all wines.

EXTRACTING THE FLAVOUR

Commercial wines are made from fermented undiluted grape-juice, perhaps with a little sugar added. But most of the fruits used in home-made wines have such a strong flavour that the pure undiluted juice obtained by pressing the fruit would produce an unpleasant wine. So instead, the juice or flavour of the fruit is extracted in one of several ways and the liquid obtained is diluted down with water to a suitable concentration. It is then called a *must*. The sugar is dissolved in the must, and yeast is added so that fermentation can begin. (Cereals, flowers and vegetables are all treated in a similar way.)

FERMENTATION

Fermentation is a natural process carried on by many kinds of fungi, bacteria, moulds and yeasts. As far as winemaking is concerned, though, fermentation specifically refers to the action of the yeast *Saccharomyces cerevisiae* on the sugar dissolved in the must.

There are two ways in which yeast can use sugar as a food. In oxygenated or *aerobic* conditions, yeast builds up a large colony of cells and digests the sugar completely. In deoxygenated or *anaerobic* conditions, the yeast does not reproduce as quickly and can only partially digest the sugar, producing alcohol and carbon dioxide gas as by-products. You can see therefore that fermentation takes place in two stages; the first or aerobic stage allows the yeast to build up a strong colony, and the second or anaerobic stage produces much alcohol. Often the first stage of fermentation takes place in a bucket or similar vessel which contains the must and usually the "pulped" material of the basic ingredients. This process helps to extract the flavour. Thus you can see that the two stages "extraction of flavour" and "fermentation" may, at least to start with, be simultaneous. After a while, however, the solids are strained from the liquid, and the liquid is poured into a demijohn or some other fermentation vessel from which the air can be excluded. As the yeast uses up the oxygen in the container, it froths and foams quite dramatically. But soon the carbon dioxide builds up, the oxygen is exhausted, and the slower anaerobic fermentation begins. When this has finished, the yeast falls to the bottom of the jar and the wine begins to clear. It is then racked (i.e. siphoned off the sediment) into a clean jar to mature.

MATURATION

A new wine often tastes rather unpleasant. But storing it for some time allows the flavour to mellow, and allows the ingredients to settle out and react with each other so as to form the subtle bouquet and flavour characteristic of a high-quality wine.

That is a brief outline of the theory; but what of the practical side of winemaking?

THE BASIC EQUIPMENT

The three stages of winemaking all require slightly different equipment. Even so, it is not necessary to spend much money. You will probably have most of the hardware listed below in your kitchen; other more sophisticated items can be added as your skill increases. Here is a list of essential equipment for making 1 gallon (4.5 litres), i.e. six standard wine bottles, of wine:

- a hard white plastic bucket of 2 gallon (9 litres) capacity, preferably with a lid or suitable close-fitting cover;
- a plastic or wooden spoon;
- a large aluminium, stainless-steel or unchipped enamel pan (if the recipe indicates that the ingredients should be boiled);
- a medium and a fine nylon mesh sheet for straining the must;
- plastic or glass fermenting vessels of 1 gallon (4.5 litres) capacity, such as the easily obtainable glass demijohn;
- a rubber bung and air-lock (see page 21);
- a plastic or nylon funnel;
- a second demijohn for storage;
- suitable bottles and stoppers for the finished wine (see page 83-4);
- four feet (1½ metres) of nylon or plastic tubing for siphoning the wine from one container to another when fermentation has finished or when bottling;
- a bottle brush for cleaning jars and bottles.

Larger quantities of wine may require the following equipment:
- a steam boiler or a fruit crusher and press;
- an electric juice-extractor;
- large fermentation vessels such as a white plastic 5 gallon (25 litres) "Brewing Bin" and glass carboys for storage of the finished wine.

Fig 1A: Essential equipment for winemaking

Plastic bucket with lid,
for mashing and pulp fermentation

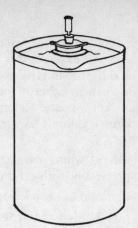

Large-scale plastic fermenter

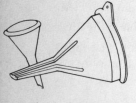

Plastic funnels

Siphon tubing and tap

NYLON STRAINING BAG

Muslin or nylon
straining bag

VARIOUS AIR-LOCKS

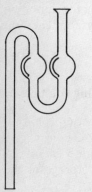

Glass bubbler

Straight-sided
plastic bubbler

Plastic
bubbler

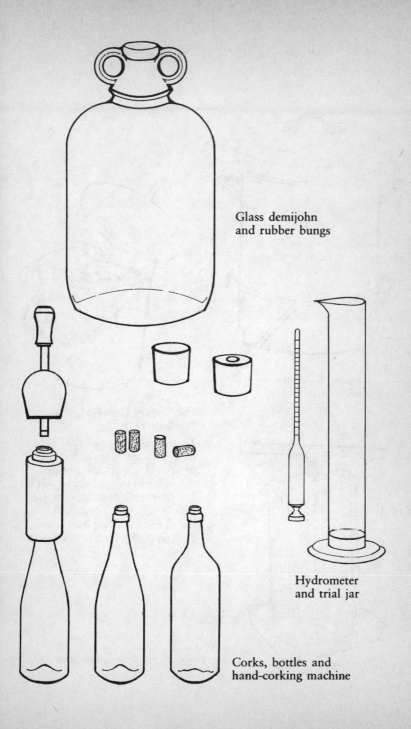

Glass demijohn
and rubber bungs

Hydrometer
and trial jar

Corks, bottles and
hand-corking machine

Fig 1B: More advanced equipment for winemaking

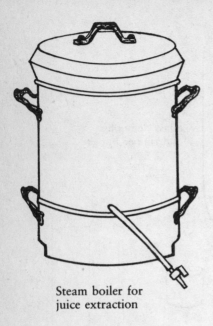

Steam boiler for juice extraction

The Walker Desmond Pulpmaker

The pulpmaster consists of a steel blade on a spindle which couples to an electric drill. It is lowered through a bearing in the bucket lid and the rotating blade pulps the fruit. The device is especially useful when making wine from hard fruit without a fruit crusher.

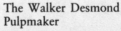

Fruit Press
(*courtesy of Walker Desmond & Sons Ltd*)

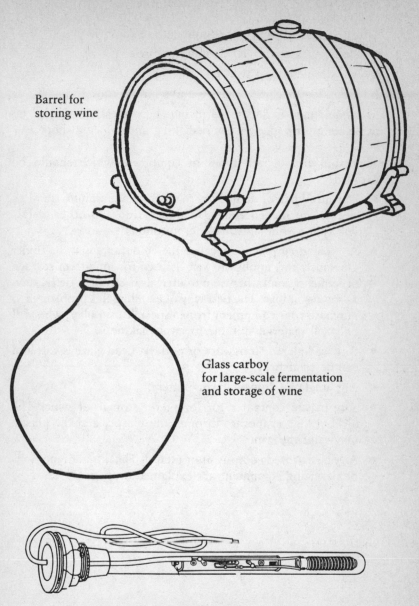

Barrel for
storing wine

Glass carboy
for large-scale fermentation
and storage of wine

Electric heater for demijohn,
with built-in thermostat and air-lock
(*courtesy of Southern Vinyards Ltd*)

Other useful but optional equipment includes:

- electric heaters for fermentation vessels;
- a hydrometer and trial jar;
- a corking machine to drive corks into bottles.

This equipment is illustrated in Fig. 1 (overleaf); it will all be available at any specialist winemaking and brewing shop.

There are also certain types of equipment which should be avoided:

- Any metal pan or utensil *not* made from aluminium, stainless steel or unchipped enamel. Copper, iron and other metals will ruin a wine and may be poisonous.

- Any coloured plastic, because the colourants may be toxic. Obviously this applies to vessels used for long-term storage or fermentation rather than to utensils used only briefly, such as spoons or jugs. The best way of avoiding this problem is to purchase your equipment from a specialist supplier, who will only sell material suitable for winemaking.

- Any lead-glazed stoneware or pottery. Lead glaze is soft and can be scratched.

- Any unglazed stoneware or pottery.

- *Any* plastic container for long-term storage of wine. The alcohol may evaporate through the plastic, and the plastic may taint the wine.

- Any unsterilized equipment or utensil. The different methods of sterilizing equipment are explained on page 23-4.

THE FERMENTATION JAR AND AIR-LOCK

With the recent astonishing growth in home winemaking as a hobby, glass demijohns have become cheaply and readily available. They are by far the safest and best vessels for the home winemaker since they do not corrode, melt, taint wine or absorb its flavour and smell. Similarly, glass carboys can be used for larger quantities of wine.

While a wine is fermenting in these containers, oxygen in the air must be excluded so as to encourage the production of alcohol. This is achieved by the use of an *air-lock*, also known as a *fermentation-lock* or *trap*. This piece of equipment prevents the outside air from gaining access to the wine and yeast, while allowing the carbon dioxide produced during fermentation to escape. It also prevents spoilage bacteria and fruit flies from entering the wine. (Small fruit flies carry the bacteria which turn wine sour or vinegary.) In this respect, of course, a thick cloth or lid over a bucket of must serves the same purpose as the air-lock on a demijohn.

All air-locks work on the same principle: a small amount of sterilizing solution is poured into the lock, the stem is pushed through a bung, and the bung is fitted to the fermentation vessel. This is illustrated in Fig. 2. Thus the external air cannot reach the wine, but the carbon dioxide gas produced by the yeast can force its way through the air-lock and escape without building up in the fermenting wine. Any air-borne bacteria which land on the air-lock will be killed by the sterilizing solution. However, most solutions lose their effectiveness after a while, and therefore need to be periodically renewed. Alternatively, a small plug of cotton wool may be inserted into the open end of the "bubbler" air-locks.

There is a large range of air-locks available; there are points for and against each model. Plastic ones are more robust but can be scratched easily. They are not cheap, either, costing almost as much as the glass bubblers. On the other hand, large plastic locks are the only ones which can cope with the gas produced by 5-gallon (25 litre) batches of wine. The glass bubbler, however,

Fig 2: Diagram showing straight-sided and bubbler air-locks, (A) correctly filled, and (B) during fermentation

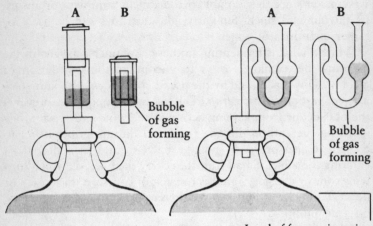

Bubble of gas forming

Bubble of gas forming

Level of fermenting wine

is ideal for small batches of wine — and highly entertaining to watch as the bubbles "blurp" through the liquid in the tube! One small defect with glass air-locks is that they are less robust than plastic ones: care must be taken when pushing them into a rubber bung or they may break and cut your hand quite badly. A drop of water on the stem acts as a useful lubricant.

With large fermentation vessels, it is possible to design one's own air-locks. A small-diameter plastic tube, for example, can be cemented into a small hole bored in the screw-top lid of a plastic container. The other end of the tube can then be submerged in a jar of sterilizing solution, through which bubbles of gas will be able to escape.

It is possible to obtain an idea of the progress of a fermentation by watching the rate at which bubbles pass through the air-lock. And of course, when fermentation is complete, no carbon dioxide gas is produced and no more bubbles pass through the air lock. (The levels on the inner and outer sides of the lock may not equalize, because the gas pressure inside and outside the jar varies differently with temperature. But so long as no gas actually passes through the lock, you know that fermentation is complete.)

Incidentally, the first stages of fermentation in a demijohn may produce so much froth and foam that the wine is actually forced right up and through the air-lock. This problem can be avoided by using a cotton-wool plug rather than a bung and air-lock for a few days until the fermentation has died down.

HYGIENE AND STERILIZATION

Before you do anything, you must be aware of the importance of hygiene in winemaking. Bacteria can infect a wine and turn it bad at any stage of production if dirty equipment or bottles are used; and the wine (not to mention all your efforts) will then be wasted.

In fact more wines are lost through off-flavours and foul tastes produced by bacterial infection than through any other cause. The most well-known infection is that of *Acetobacter*, which turns wine into vinegar (acetic acid) by a process of acetification. The wine can then only be poured away or used for cooking.

Similarly, "wild" yeasts abound on fruit and in the air. Unlike cultured wine yeasts, these yeasts can only produce small amounts of alcohol; they also taint a wine with all kinds of unpleasant flavours. Thus their presence in a wine is highly undesirable.

In practical terms, this means that all the ingredients, utensils and equipment which come into contact with your wine at any time must be first washed or rinsed and then sterilized. This includes even small items which might be overlooked, such as spoons, straining bag, hydrometer and siphon tube. Otherwise sooner or later you'll produce an infected wine with a foul taste and smell.

There are several effective methods of sterilization:

1) *Boiling water.* The water must be poured over the ingredients or equipment whilst it is actually boiling or it won't work effectively. DO NOT pour boiling water over or into cool glass or it will inevitably break.

2) *Household bleach solution.* A very effective sterilizing agent is household bleach, diluted at the rate of one cupful to a gallon (4.5 litres) of water. This solution is suitable for sterilizing plastic and glass equipment only, as it corrodes metal. Jars and bottles can be filled to the neck, while smaller pieces of equipment can be placed in a bucket containing the solution. In both cases, leaving the equipment overnight should ensure it is thoroughly sterilized. Be sure to rinse everything before you start, though, as any traces of bleach would certainly spoil the wine. The bleach solution can be used several times.

If you decide to use this method of sterilization, do remember that bleach can be dangerous, so keep it off your hands and, above all, don't leave it where children can get at it.

3) *Milton.* Products such as Milton, which are designed for sterilizing babies' feeding equipment, are very suitable for use with winemaking equipment. Follow the instructions on the bottle or packet.

4) *Chempro SDP.* This product cleans and sterilizes at the same time and can therefore be a useful time-saver. It is certainly effective (it is used by breweries) when used as directed on the packet.

5) *Sodium metabisulphite or Campden tablets.* (The latter are simply a compressed form of metabisulphite powder.) Metabisulphite dissolves in water to form a solution of sulphur dioxide gas; the sulphur dioxide sterilizes any equipment with which it comes into contact.

When using either sulphite or Campden tablets, follow the instructions provided. Usually one teaspoonful of sulphite powder or eight Campden tablets — these need to be crushed before use — are dissolved in one pint (600 ml) of cold water. (Hot water drives off the sulphur dioxide gas before it has had time to kill any bacteria present.) The potency of the sterilizing solution can be increased by adding a pinch of citric acid crystals to the water. DO NOT breathe the fumes!

Like bleach solution, sulphite is only suitable for non-metallic equipment. When sterilizing a jar or bottle, the sterilizing solution does not need to fill the container, but it should be shaken and rolled around the surface several times so as to cover the entire area of the vessel. A solution of sulphite can be used more than once if it is kept in a screw-topped jar or bottle with no air-space. Always check the potency of the solution by sniffing (very cautiously) for sulphur dioxide gas. If you can't detect it, make up a new solution.

Once a jar or bottle has been sterilized, it can be kept sterile by corking it with about half an inch (10 mm) of solution in the bottom.

If you are preparing a must or working with a fermenting wine, all sterilized equipment should be well drained, or rinsed with sterile (i.e. boiled and cooled) water before use. Otherwise the traces of sulphite may inhibit the wine yeast, and if that happens, a hydrogen sulphide (bad egg) smell may develop. Similarly, if the sulphite used for sterilizing equipment gets into a finished wine, it may spoil the colour, so rinse out any jars and bottles before you use them.

THE TECHNIQUE OF MAKING WINE

In the next sections, I describe in much more detail the entire procedure of making wine, and explain the roles of all the different additives recommended in the recipes. The sections are set out in a way designed to correspond roughly to the actual sequence of operations involved in making a wine at home, beginning with the different methods of extracting the flavour

25

from the ingredients. The first part of the book includes a list of problems and remedies (pages 89-92).

SELECTING THE INGREDIENTS AND EXTRACTING THE FLAVOUR

These are the main types of ingredient from which wine can be made:

- fruit — fresh, canned, dried, bottled, frozen
- fruit juices
- flowers — fresh, dried
- vegetables — fresh
- cereals.

You can see immediately that there is an enormous range of materials available for winemaking at any time of year. Exactly where you start depends on a number of factors, including the season of the year, the time and money you wish to spend on selecting and preparing your ingredients, and your personal tastes and preferences. Generally, fruit wines are by far the most popular, followed by flower, vegetable and cereal wines, probably in that order. This does not mean that fruit wines are necessarily better than, say, vegetable wines: there are simply fewer vegetables suitable for good winemaking than there are fruits.

As I have explained, the basis of winemaking is to extract the flavour of the main ingredient in such a way that when sugar is added, the liquid produced can be fermented into wine. There are many ways of achieving the extraction of flavour; they may be listed as follows:

- direct fermentation of fruit juice diluted with water
- boiling the fruit or vegetables in water

- hot-water extraction
- pulp fermentation
- carbonic maceration
- infusion
- sugar extraction.

1. DIRECT FERMENTATION

Pure fruit juices can be bought easily and cheaply. There are the well-known varieties of apple, orange, pineapple and grapefruit as well as more exotic varieties such as passion fruit juice. If you use these juices as the basis for making wine — and they give excellent results with no fuss or mess — buy those which contain no preservative (this might affect the wine yeast) and no added sugar (this would affect the amount of sugar needed in the recipe).

Besides fruit juices, concentrated fruit syrups such as blackcurrant Ribena and rosehip syrup are also useful for winemaking. Suitable recipes are included in the second section of this book.

There are various ways of extracting fruit juice at home. The most obvious is to chop or crush the fruit and then to press it. Small presses for the amateur winemaker are not hard to obtain; they range from small models suitable for single gallons (4.5 litres) of wine to large presses capable of taking large batches of fruit at one go. Any winemaking store should have details of the different sorts of equipment available. Two points to note: the fruit or fruit pieces should be wrapped in cloth (muslin) bags before pressing; and the same quantity of fruit will be required whether one presses it to extract the juice or uses a completely different method such as pulp fermentation (see 4 below).

At least to start with, the average winemaker will probably have neither the resources nor the desire to buy or borrow a fruit crusher and press. Suitable alternatives include electric juice extractors or steam juice extractors. The electric machines are certainly convenient and efficient with hard fruits (although not suitable for soft or citrus fruits), but they are also rather expensive. If you do decide to make the investment, try to ensure that you buy a machine which ejects pulp and juice separately.

27

Many fresh fruits and juices turn brown when the fruit is cut or damaged, in the same way that an apple discolours when it is cut in half. This browning spoils the taste of the wine, but it can be prevented by dissolving one Campden tablet in each gallon of juice or must, or by dropping the crushed fruit into sulphited water, i.e. water containing one dissolved Campden tablet per gallon (or 4.5 litres). This will also help to destroy bacteria and wild yeasts. But always remember that whenever Campden tablets are added to a must, twenty-four hours should elapse before the wine yeast is added. By this time the sulphur dioxide will have dispersed and there is no danger of the yeast being inhibited by it.

The enzymes responsible for browning are destroyed by hot or boiling water. Thus canned fruits or fruit juices in sealed cartons, which have been heated to sterilize them, will not brown. Equally, a steam extractor produces sterile juice which will not discolour. The steam extractor consists of a lower pan of boiling water and an upper pan containing the fruit, all enclosed. The steam breaks down the tissue of the fruit or vegetables and the juice runs out of a special outlet. "Steamers" seem to be regarded as a rather old-fashioned way of preparing fruit or vegetables, but they are efficient and effective. Once again, any specialist winemaking shop should be able to supply details.

2. BOILING

Some ingredients, notably vegetables and bananas, may be boiled in water until they are tender but not mushy. The liquid is then strained off the solid matter, diluted as required, and the yeast and other ingredients introduced for fermentation. In fact all vegetable wines are prepared in this way.

3. HOT WATER EXTRACTION

Some winemakers heat red fruits, especially blackcurrants, sloes and elderberries, in water at 70°–80°C (160°–175°F) for about fifteen minutes. This softens and sterilizes the fruit and also extracts the maximum amount of flavour while reducing the harshness of the fruit tannin (see page 40) which is sometimes quite concentrated in red fruit — especially elderberries. After heating, the fruit pulp is pressed gently and the liquid strained off, after which it is made up to the required volume and fermented. In my opinion, all hard, sour or unripe fruit benefits from being heated in this way, even if a pulp fermentation is planned (see below), since it softens the fruit and aids the extraction of flavour.

4. PULP FERMENTATION

This is one of the most common and popular methods of extracting the flavour from winemaking ingredients, and is the method outlined in the majority of recipes in this book. So what does it entail?

The basic ingredients are placed in a fermentation bin or bucket and then sterilized. This is done by pouring boiling water over them and ensuring that any fruit is crushed so that the boiling water reaches every part of the material. The idea is to kill any wild yeasts and bacteria which might otherwise spoil the wine. After the boiling water has been added, the bin or bucket is covered and allowed to cool to 20°–25°C (68°–75°F) before the yeast and certain other ingredients are mixed in.

Despite what you may read elsewhere, the addition of one or two Campden tablets to a must is *not* a totally effective method of sterilization. Boiling water should be used if at all possible. However, if for any reason the wine yeast cannot immediately be added to a cool sterilized must, dissolving one or two Campden tablets in each gallon (4.5 litres) will help to prevent infection by air-borne bacteria; obviously the must should be kept covered with a non-porous sheet or lid and, as explained in section 1, twenty-four hours should elapse before the yeast is added.

In some cases, boiling water cannot be used because of its harmful effects on the basic ingredients. For example, flowers, especially dried ones, are ruined by the use of boiling water, which drives off all the volatile oils and essences that contribute to the special character of flower wines. And pouring boiling water over cereal grains produces a sticky, starchy mass. In such cases, hot water and/or Campden tablets must be accepted as adequate sterilizing agents. The tablets are dissolved in the must when it is cool (as already explained, they are rendered useless if added to hot or boiling water) and the fermentation bin is covered and left for twenty-four hours before the yeast is added.

Fermentation begins soon after the yeast is added and continues in the presence of the fruit, cereal or flower "pulp" for a certain period of time, the length of which depends on the nature of the ingredients. During this period, the yeast multiplies vigorously and establishes a strong colony. It also produces a small amount of alcohol which leaches out the flavour, colour and body of the ingredients. To help this extraction, and to reduce the risk of infection, the fermentation bin is covered and the fruit "cap" (which rises to the surface because of the gas produced during fermentation) is stirred into the liquid twice daily.

When enough colour and flavour have been leached into the wine, the liquid is strained off the pulp. Sugar is added if necessary, the liquid is poured into a demijohn and topped up with cool boiled water. Then the air-lock is fitted and the anaerobic fermentation begins.

5. CARBONIC MACERATION

This is one of the newest and least well-known winemaking techniques. It was developed in California, where commercial winemaking is now a major industry. The Californian vineyards keep whole bunches of red grapes in an atmosphere of carbon dioxide for one week. While in this atmosphere, each grape is isolated from all the others, and chemical reactions rather different to those of a normal pulp fermentation take place in the skin of the grape. Those elements of the grape which provide flavour and colour dissolve into the juice, but the harsh tannin (see page 40) is not extracted as it would be in a pulp fermentation. After a week, the grapes are crushed and pressed and the juice is separated and fermented in the normal way.

Carbonic maceration can be successfully adapted for the home winemaker. When used with red fruits such as plums, elderberries and blackberries it is claimed to give the full flavour of the fruit with a fresh taste and without the need to mature the wine for years while the harsh flavour of the tannin mellows out.

And the technique is simple enough. First, the fruit is washed, any bad parts are removed, and it is soaked in sulphited water for a few hours. It is then placed in an almost airtight container with as small an air space as possible. Any air in the container is displaced by carbon dioxide produced through the action of yeast. One pint (600 ml) of yeast starter (see page 45) containing about 4oz (110 g) of dissolved sugar is required for each gallon (4.5 litres) of volume in the container. The yeast starter should be poured down the side of the container so that it rests on the bottom.

The container is kept at 20°C (68°F) for one week, after which the fruit is crushed and pressed to extract the juice. The juice is made up to the required volume in the normal way and fermented out under an air-lock. Obviously the technique is only suitable for certain fruits, i.e. smooth-skinned berries and all tree fruits with single stones. Otherwise it seems to be a technique with which the adventurous amateur may find it is well worth experimenting. (Note: this technique is not a traditional one and so has not been described in the recipes in this book.)

6. INFUSION

This is an alternative to the use of hot water techniques for flower wines. It is designed to preserve the delicate scents and oils which are responsible for the bouquet and flavour of flower wines. Basically, the flowers are soaked in water for one or two days to extract their aroma and character, and the infused extract is then added to a fermenting must made with grape juice. This is used because flowers impart only flavour and scent. To ensure a wine-like quality in the finished drink, a suitable fruit base is required.

An alternative technique recommended by some authors is simply to soak the flowers in a fermenting must after the initial violent ferment has died down. (It is said that the rapid escape of carbon dioxide in the first stage of fermentation can carry off the volatile scents and oils from the flowers.) The recommended method is to place the flowers in a suitable bag made of linen, muslin or nylon mesh and to hang this in the fermenting must. This avoids any problems of separating the solids from the liquid. Clearly there is room for experiment here, and the techniques described in the recipes should be regarded as suggestions rather than rules.

7. SUGAR EXTRACTION

This is a method of flavour extraction originally designed for use with rhubarb, which contains unpleasant oxalic acid that dissolves easily in hot water. However, the method could certainly be used with other fruits.

The fruit is washed, dried and sliced into a bucket. It is then covered with the sugar specified in the recipe. After 24–36 hours, the sugar will have sucked out the juice and dissolved in it to form a thick syrupy liquid. This can be strained into a demijohn, diluted and fermented at once. The pulp can be washed with water to remove any flavour remaining on the fruit.

SELECTING FRUIT AND OTHER INGREDIENTS

One golden rule of home winemaking is that the best quality fruit produces the best quality wine. Select your ingredients carefully, choosing sound ripe fruit wherever possible. Wash it before use, and cut out any soft or brown patches. Certain fruits, such as gooseberries, blackcurrants and pineapples, need "topping and tailing" before use. The stones may be left in smaller fruits — it would be an impossible job to take them out — but are best removed from plums and peaches.

If *any* stones are cracked, the kernels will impart a pronounced and irremovable almond flavour to the wine; so do not use electric pulpers or juicing machines on this kind of fruit! Similarly, the pips of citrus fruits and grapes do not affect a wine — provided they are not crushed. You must, however, be very careful to exclude all citrus fruit pith, for this imparts a very bitter taste to a wine. The same is true of the flesh of the *grapefruit*.

Sometimes fruit looks ripe when it is in fact still quite acidic. Consider damsons, for example. Very often the damsons bought at greengrocers' shops are under-ripe and acidic, even though they look black. Such fruit will make a better wine if it is left to ripen in a dry, clean place for a few weeks. If you do use fruit when it is hard and slightly sour, it is a good idea to boil it for a few minutes to soften the tissue and ameliorate the acidity. You can then pulp ferment in the normal way. The importance of using ripe fruit is illustrated by the somewhat unpleasant taste produced in a peach wine made with unripe peaches. The only exception to this rule is that unripe gooseberries are far preferable to soft, ripe ones. This is because the strong flavour of the ripe fruit is too pronounced in a finished wine.

One final word about fresh fruit — berries are best gathered on a dry day, if possible. This is because they absorb water and swell when wet. Thus on a wet day one has proportionately more water and less flavour for a given weight of fruit than on a dry day. This problem can be avoided by adding extra fruit if it has been gathered on a wet day.

Canned and bottled fruit is of course sterile and soft; it can be poured directly into a fermentation bin and pulp fermented without any preparation. Similar reasoning applies to commercially produced *fruit juices, concentrates and syrups*. However, if you have prepared a juice yourself by pressing fresh fruit, it is a wise precaution to dissolve two Campden tablets in each gallon (4.5 litres) of juice or must and leave it for twenty-four hours before adding any yeast.

Dried fruit needs careful preparation. Although the high sugar content prevents decay during storage, there will still be many bacteria and spoilage organisms on the fruit. Before use in winemaking, it needs to be washed in cold, running water and then boiled (some recipes call for this) or soaked in sulphited water for twenty-four hours. It can then be treated like fresh fruit. Some dried fruits, in particular sultanas and raisins, are sometimes lightly coated with oil before they are packed, to prevent them sticking together during storage. This oil must be removed by washing the fruit in hot water, otherwise it will float on the surface of the must and wine.

The same guidelines apply to *vegetables* as apply to fresh fruit. Thus the first point, as before, is to use good quality ingredients. Scrub the vegetables well (but do not peel), remove "tops and tails", cut out any bad parts and chop before boiling. Only the liquid is used in making wine; the chunks are discarded.

Flowers, like berries, are best gathered on a dry day. Individual blossoms like elderflowers can be combed off the stalks using a comb with widely spaced teeth. Other flowers such as dandelion and coltsfoot need to be plucked off the green stems and calyces (the outer green part of the flower) as much as possible. More detailed instructions are included in the relevant recipes.

Dried flowers are certainly more convenient, in that one is spared the chore of picking them; however, be careful to remove all foreign matter such as stones or sticks from the petals, and rinse them in sulphited water and drain before use. *Never* use boiling water on flowers, especially dried ones, or you will simply produce a foul-smelling liquid quite unsuitable for making wine.

Cereals can be obtained as either whole grain or flakes. I recommend the use of whole grain, which is cleaner and easier to use. Since all the flavour of the cereal grain is concentrated in the outer husk or epidermis, it is not necessary to mince the grain as is sometimes suggested. Wash the grain well to remove dust and insecticides or preservatives, then pour on hot water to extract the flavour. Full details can be found in the relevant recipes.

STRAINING

The success of winemaking depends to a large extent on the care with which the liquid is strained from the fruit pulp or other ingredients. The aim is to allow as little solid matter as possible into the demijohn for the anaerobic fermentation. Thus one should avoid squeezing pulp through a straining mesh or bag, since this will purée the material and allow it to pass through into the wine. In fact only the gentlest pressure should be exerted on the solid material. It is far better to roll the pulp around a straining mesh and wash it with water than to squeeze it in an attempt to extract every last remnant of flavour. Coarse, medium and fine nylon mesh sheets ideal for straining solids from liquids can be obtained from winemaking stores.

Do not confuse *straining* with *filtering*. To strain a wine must is to remove the coarser particles or chunks of solid matter from the liquid; yeast and other such tiny particles pass easily through a straining bag. To filter a wine is to pass it through a very fine "sieve" with microscopic holes, the idea being to remove *all* suspended matter and leave a brilliantly clear liquid. (See page 69.)

OTHER WINEMAKING INGREDIENTS

WATER

Ordinary tap water is best for winemaking. If the supply is known to be treated, as in Britain, one could even take a chance and use it straight from the tap. However, it is wisest to boil all water before use; this will drive off any chlorine and ensure that it really is sterile. (Incidentally, this problem of excess chlorine in the water supply seems to have become much worse in recent years. In some areas of Britain, the level of chlorine is apparently so high that it spoils both the colour and taste of the wine unless the water is treated first! For small batches of wine, it is a simple enough matter to boil the water before use; however, for 5- or 10-gallon fermentations (25 or 50 litres) you will find it more convenient to buy a small water purifier. These are filter devices which clip on to the tap and remove the chlorine by chemical action. They are not hard to find, and can be a boon if you are plagued by this particular problem. One winemaking firm which may be able to help is Southern Vinyards of Hove, East Sussex.)

Rain water and well water are not recommended for winemaking. There is no good reason to use them, anyway, since the hardness or softness of water has no effect whatsoever on winemaking. Distilled water will not work at all since it lacks the essential "trace" elements necessary for the growth of a yeast colony.

PECTIC ENZYME*

Fruit and vegetable matter contains a gummy carbohydrate substance called pectin between the cell walls. This pectin is, in effect, the "cement" which holds the cells of the fruit together (this glue-like property makes pectin suitable for use in jam-making — it ensures a firm set). However, pectin released by the preparation of fruit or vegetables for winemaking can cause a cloudiness in the finished wine. Fortunately this problem can be overcome by the use of a commercially prepared pectin-destroying enzyme which is added to the *cool* must at the beginning of fermentation.

Another advantage is that the use of a pectin-destroying enzyme also seems to improve the flavour.

Preparations of pectic enzyme will remove any pectin released into the must during preparation; they are available under different brand names, such as Pectolase, Pectinol, Pectolytic enzyme, Pectic enzyme and so on. In addition there is a specialized preparation known as *Rohament P*, which releases the colour and flavour of chopped fruit. This is especially useful when one is making wine from hard fruits like apples without a fruit press. However, Rohament P will not, on its own, produce a pectin-free must, so it should be used in conjunction with one of the pectic enzymes mentioned above.

If a recipe specifies "pectic enzyme" and it is added in accordance with the instructions on the packet, the finished wine should be clear and bright. If you do happen to produce a wine with a haze, you can easily test for pectin as described on page 82. If the test proves positive, a double dose of enzyme can be added to the finished wine. However, pectic enzyme is best added to a must and not to a finished wine, in which its action is less effective.

DIASTASE OR FUNGAL AMYLASE

Some ingredients — notably cereals and root vegetables —

*Enzymes are chemical compounds produced by living cells. They are responsible for the conversion of one substance to another, e.g. sugar to alcohol during fermentation. However, an extract of enzyme can work independently of living tissue.

contain starch, and this can, like pectin, cause a haze in a finished wine. The addition of the starch-destroying enzyme *diastase* (sometimes known as fungal amylase) will prevent this. The recipes clearly indicate when it is required; use it as directed on the packet.

ACID

The acidity of a wine must plays a major part in determining the quality of a finished wine. A serious lack of acid makes a wine taste distinctly medicinal (a flavour which cannot be removed); a slight lack of acid makes a wine taste dull, flat or insipid; too much acid makes a wine sharp and sour to taste. Acid is also important in the development of good bouquet in a wine. During fermentation and storage, the acids react with the alcohol to produce a set of volatile chemical compounds known as *esters*. It is these compounds which are chiefly responsible for the good bouquet of a wine; without enough acid in the must, they do not develop.

But besides the obvious advantages mentioned above, the correct level of acidity is important in other ways. Yeast needs an acidic environment for effective fermentation; and the correct level of acid in a wine helps to inhibit the activity of spoilage bacteria — and so acts as a natural preservative during fermentation and storage.

There are three main acids used by the home winemaker: citric, tartaric and malic.

Citric acid is the acid of citrus fruits. It always has been, and still is, the most useful acid for home winemakers. This is because its taste is quite acceptable and it effectively provides an acidic environment for the yeast. Old recipes specify lemons or oranges as a source of citric acid; newer ones indicate the required quantity of citric acid crystals. Using the crystallized form of the acid is simple, convenient and easy: the crystals dissolve readily in water.

Tartaric acid is the main acid found in grapes and, of course, grape-juice concentrates. It is available to the home winemaker as tartaric acid crystals. Its great advantage is that any excess acid will precipitate out as insoluble potassium tartrate during the later stages of maturation. Some red fruit recipes seem to be improved by the use of tartaric rather than citric acid, but this is not a factor of any great importance. Certain authorities recommend the use of a 50/50 blend of tartaric/citric acid so as to obtain the advantages of both types of acid. This mixture substitutes for an equal quantity of either citric or tartaric acid.

Note: potassium tartrate also tends to precipitate out if a wine is cooled. This is not a problem with red wines, which are served at room temperature; however, tartrate hazes can develop in a white wine which is chilled before serving, and so tartaric acid is best avoided in white table-wine recipes. (If a red wine should happen to throw some crystals, for example during storage in a cool place, you can easily decant it off the crystals before you serve it.)

Malic acid is another acid naturally present in the grape, and also in apples. Too much malic acid can impart a sharp and sour taste which is not entirely acceptable in a good quality wine. Fortunately that problem only occurs with very acidic apples, and it can be dealt with artificially by adding potassium carbonate (see page 89) or naturally by a malo-lactic fermentation.

A malo-lactic fermentation is quite a rare event. It is not caused by yeast, but by the lactic acid bacteria which can convert malic acid to *lactic acid*. When it happens, a winemaker may be puzzled to find that his wine appears to be fermenting very slowly for a long time after the yeast has used up all the available sugar. In such a case, the normal yeast fermentation has indeed ended, but has been superseded by a fermentation of malic to lactic acid with associated production of carbon dioxide. Apart from the fact that it is annoying to have a finished wine fermenting during storage, a malo-lactic fermentation is generally regarded as a good thing, because lactic acid has a pleasant taste and contributes to a good bouquet.

Lactic acid can be purchased — with some difficulty — as a solution in water. One teaspoonful added to each gallon (4.5 litres) of wine must produces a significant improvement in a wine's bouquet after storage. One teaspoon of 50 per cent lactic acid solution replaces half a teaspoon of citric or tartaric acid crystals.

CHECKING THE ACIDITY

Although you can obtain satisfactory results by following a recipe, obviously one problem is that fruits do vary in acidity from year to year — particularly depending on the amount of sunshine in a season. You may therefore wish to check the acidity of your wine must and adjust the quantity of acid used in the recipe accordingly. Clearly one has to carry out such a test when one has compounded the full volume of the must, for dilution of the must will also dilute the acid.

The simplest way of checking acidity is to use pH indicator paper (pH is a measure of acidity: pH 7 is neutral, less than pH 7 is acidic, and over pH 7 is alkaline.) The indicator paper is simply dipped into the wine must. It then changes colour and can be compared to a standard colour chart which shows the corresponding acidity.

An alternative method is to use titration or a wine acidity test kit. Full instructions are supplied with this equipment, but the principle is very simple: the acid in a small measured volume of must reacts with standard sodium hydroxide solution containing an indicator which changes colour at a certain pH. The volume of sodium hydroxide solution required to bring this change about can be converted to an acidity reading for the must.

In general, wine musts should have an acidity of between pH 3 and 4; pH 3.3 is the figure usually quoted for a table wine. However, a wine which is finished sweet and strong needs slightly more acid, say pH 3.1. These figures are equivalent to an acidity level of about 5 parts per thousand (ppt) for a table wine must and 7 ppt for a strong, sweet wine must.

If you think your must is too acid (as it may be with certain fruits, notably blackcurrants and citrus fruit) it is wiser to wait until the wine is finished before making any adjustments. Remember that you can always remove acidity, but a wine whose flavour is spoilt because it contained too little acid will be irretrievable. If you do need to reduce a wine's acidity, proprietary brands of "wine acid reduction solution" are available; alternatively, you can use potassium carbonate solution. This is explained more fully in the section "Faults and remedies" on page 89.

Another method of adjusting the acidity of a must which one sometimes sees recommended is the addition of precipitated chalk (calcium carbonate). I have tried this myself and found it to be unsatisfactory for several reasons. First of all, chalk is not soluble, which means that the must has to be stirred until the excess acid is sufficiently neutralized. Next, the must has to be left undisturbed until the chalk has settled out — sometimes one even has to filter it. Lastly, the must needs re-acidifying with citric acid or lemon juice. All this is tedious enough, but much worse is the fact that the colour and flavour of a wine can be spoiled by the chalk. If, despite these problems, you wish to try the technique, ½ to 1 ounce (15–30 grams) of chalk should be enough for even the most acidic must. However, my advice is to avoid this procedure if at all possible.

Another technique for adjusting the acidity of a must or a finished wine which can cause more problems than it cures is adding water to dilute the acid. In the case of a must, you will also dilute the flavour, and in a finished wine you will dilute both flavour and alcohol content. Finally, remember that most wines, no matter how acidic or astringent, will mellow with keeping.

TANNIN

Tannin is a compound derived from the skin and pips of fruit. It helps to balance the flavour of all wines and provides a sharpness or "bite" without which a wine is dull and insipid. Red berries and fruits such as grapes, elderberries and bilberries contain a great deal of tannin; obviously flower, vegetable, cereal and white fruit or juice wines will contain little or no tannin. To make up this deficiency, powdered grape tannin may be added to a must. The powder clots if added straight to a must, so it needs to be creamed into a smooth paste with a little water before being well mixed into the bulk. The quantity required is indicated in each of the recipes; in general, this varies from one-eighth to half a teaspoonful.

Older recipes indicate the use of strong tea, which is a rich source of tannin. The quantities vary from a tablespoonful to a cupful — which is one reason why modern recipes, with a specifically defined quantity of a uniform substance such as grape tannin, are a considerable improvement.

Wine with tannin will keep much better than wine without. However, in general, the more tannin a wine contains, the longer it will need in storage before the flavour has mellowed to a pleasant drinkability. This is one reason why rich red grape wines (and some home-made wines) made with large quantities of fruit need to be stored for years before use. During this storage and maturation, the subtle chemical changes which take place in the developing wine include the precipitation of excess tannin.

The optimum storage time for a home-made red wine, using an average amount of fruit, will probably be about six months. This does not, of course, mean that the wine cannot be drunk before this! However, some red fruits — for example, elderberries — contain a great deal of tannin and may require even longer storage. Fortunately the storage times can be kept to a minimum by avoiding a lengthy pulp fermentation (which extracts the tannin from the skin of the fruit) and using the minimum quantity of fruit. Other useful techniques which avoid the extraction of too much tannin include hot water extraction, carbonic maceration, and, in the case of elderberries, the use of juice pressed from the fresh berries rather than the whole fruit.

I shall return to the subject of tannin in later sections; for the moment, three points only. First, if a wine is found to contain too little tannin, more can be added later at any stage. Secondly, it is useful for each individual winemaker to learn how much tannin suits his palate and to adjust the recipes accordingly. Thirdly, too much tannin will mask the flavour of delicate fruits such as peach and pineapple (although this factor is taken into account in the recipes).

YEAST AND YEAST NUTRIENT

Yeast is a single-celled fungus-like organism (scientifically called *Saccharomyces*, meaning "sugar fungus") which ferments sugar to alcohol under deoxygenated, or anaerobic conditions. There are several types of yeast, some of which are much more suitable for winemaking than others.

To start with, brewer's or baker's yeast (*Sacch. cerevisiae*) should be avoided. In its fresh form, this type has an unpleasant flavour which can be imparted to a wine. In its dried form it works reasonably well during fermentation, but it consists of much smaller cells than the genuine wine yeast (*Saccharomyces cerevisiae ellipsoideus*) and so does not readily form a sediment when fermentation is complete. Clearing the wine can then be a problem.

Genuine wine yeasts are derived from the yeasts which occur naturally on the skin of grapes as bloom. There are both *general-purpose* and *specific varieties* of wine yeast available in dried granulated form, or as compressed tablets, or as liquid cultures on agar.

GENERAL-PURPOSE YEASTS

These yeasts are a mixture of strains selected to give the best all-round performance. This means, really, that they have four desirable characteristics:

1) *They ferment rapidly and vigorously.*   No one wants to wait months for the finished product! However, it is worth remembering that rapid fermentation also depends on a good supply of yeast nutrient and vitamins (see below), and a stable, consistent temperature at the correct level.

2) *They have a tolerance to high levels of alcohol.*   Although alcohol is exactly what the winemaker wants in his wine, to the yeast alcohol is nothing more than a poisonous waste product of its own metabolism. And at a certain level of alcohol, which varies between different types of yeast, the yeast is simply inhibited or killed. General-purpose yeasts can ferment up to about 16% or 17% alcohol by volume — more than enough for table wines.

3) *They rapidly form a firm sediment when fermentation is complete.*   As I have mentioned, one of the problems with baker's yeast is that the cells are small and do not drop rapidly

out of suspension when the ferment has finished. This problem does not arise with wine yeasts, although the "dropping out" can be speeded up by moving the wine into a cool place. Furthermore, the sediment is firm and therefore remains undisturbed when the wine is siphoned off (racked).

4) *They do not impart off-flavours to wine.*   General thinking used to be: "siphon the wine off the yeast sediment as soon as possible when fermentation has finished" — this in case the yeast began to decay and imparted a bad smell or taste to the wine. Although one should still rack as soon as possible, the danger of a good general-purpose yeast tainting a wine during or after fermentation seems quite small.

All in all, therefore, the requirements of the average wine (and winemaker) are fulfilled by the general-purpose yeasts; the two most well known are C.W.E.'s Formula 67 and Unican's Super Yeast. However, any good-quality brand will successfully carry out any task asked of it — *except* dry sherry and sparkling wine production (see pages 173 and 176).

SPECIFIC YEAST VARIETIES

Besides the general-purpose yeasts, there is available to the home winemaker a range of specific yeasts labelled Bordeaux, Burgundy, Port, Graves, Champagne and so on. These are cultures of different strains of *S. cerevisiae*. You may wonder why so many different types of wine yeast are available if the general-purpose yeasts are so satisfactory. This is an interesting question which deserves full discussion.

The first point to be absolutely clear about is that the use of a specific wine yeast does not produce a wine of the corresponding type. This is fairly obvious. In fact the idea underlying the use of specific yeasts is that different musts produce an environment which is more suitable to certain strains of yeasts than to others. Thus, for example, a strong peach-based must is said to favour a Sauternes yeast, and so on. The reasoning is that the composition of these musts resembles the composition of the corresponding grape and hence the type of wine from which the yeast was originally derived.

In addition, it is claimed that each type of yeast has a slightly different metabolism and therefore produces a slightly different flavour and bouquet in the finished wine. But would anyone except an expert notice these differences? One way of finding out for yourself would be to ferment two similar musts with different yeasts and to compare the finished wines.

My own opinion is that a correctly balanced and constituted must is far more important than the variety of yeast used. If you have this, then using specific varieties of yeast is, as it were, nothing more than fine-tuning. However, two cases where it is *essential* that specific varieties of yeast are used is in the making of dry sherry and sparkling wine. This is explained later in the book. Perhaps the only other time when the amateur need question whether he should use a specific type is in the production of strong sweet dessert wines: Sauternes and Port yeasts are best for white and red wines, respectively, of this type.

Note that if you wanted to produce a wine of the highest possible alcoholic strength, for example to make a mock port or sherry without having to add any extra alcohol, you would have to use a Madeira, Tokay or Sherry yeast, since those have the highest alcohol tolerance of all.

To recap, then, I would suggest the following scheme:

Type of wine	Type of yeast	Alcohol tolerance
White dessert wines	Sauternes	(15%)
Red dessert wines	Port	(15%)
Sparkling wines	Champagne	(up to 14%)
"Sherry"	Sherry flor	(up to 18%)
"Port"	Madeira	(up to 18%)
High alcohol production	Madeira or Tokay	(up to 18%)
All others	General purpose	(16%–17%)

YEAST NUTRIENT

Just as plants need fertilizer, so yeast needs certain chemicals — in particular, nitrogen (N), phosphorus (P) and sulphur (S) — for vigorous growth and effective fermentation. Some ingredients

44

provide all these elements, but most country wine musts are deficient in one or more. To overcome this, you can add a yeast nutrient preparation when preparing the must. The best nutrient is a mixture of ammonium phosphate [$(NH_4)_3 PO_4$] and ammonium sulphate [$(NH_4)_2 SO_4$] crystals. This is included in some wine yeast preparations; if not, simply dissolve one level teaspoon of the mixture in the cool must or yeast starter (see below). The nutrient compound is destroyed by hot water.

THE YEAST STARTER

Wine yeast preparations of any type, whether they are dried granulated forms in hermetically sealed packets, or compressed tablets, or liquid cultures, are all dormant when they are purchased and need to be reactivated before they can be added to a must. (I recommend that you buy the dried granulated form in sealed foil bags. These have a shelf life of three or more years; liquid cultures and tablets are acceptable if fresh, but after a comparatively short time will contain so few live cells that the start-up of your fermentation could be seriously hindered.)

Current thinking on the question of fermentation is that it is inadvisable to add any yeast — even the granulated sort — directly to a wine must. If this is done, there is a considerable delay before a strong colony can build up, and infection with spoilage bacteria then becomes a real possibility. This can be avoided by activating the yeast in a so-called starter bottle and then adding the starter to the must. This ensures that the yeast begins to ferment the sugar in the must almost at once, and the carbon dioxide which is produced then acts as a barrier over the surface and helps to exclude bacteria.

A yeast starter is best made up in a sterile screw-top glass jar or bottle — a litre fruit-juice bottle is ideal. Here is the method:

1. Boil up ¼ pint (300 ml) of water containing:
   2 oz (60 g) sugar, ¼ teaspoon citric acid and ¼ pint (150 ml) of the must;

   or 2 oz (60 g) sugar and ¼ pint (150 ml) of orange juice;

   or 2 oz (60 g) sugar, ¼ teaspoon citric acid and 1 tablespoon liquid malt extract.

45

Note: these quantities of sugar and acid should be deducted from the amounts specified in the recipes.

2. Allow to cool to about 20°–25°C (68°–77°F) with jar covered.

3. Disperse yeast culture into the liquid, adding a nutrient preparation if necessary.

4. Place the lid loosely on the jar and leave it at room temperature for at least twelve hours. This will produce a good, strong yeast colony ready to ferment the must.

5. Disperse the yeast into the must. Fermentation will start shortly.

Many books or instructions indicate a small volume of starter (say, one cupful) and a preparation time of only six hours. But using the larger quantities and longer preparation times indicated above is a much more practical idea and can only be beneficial.

VITAMIN SUPPLEMENTS

The growth of a yeast colony is aided, as I have explained, by the addition of yeast nutrient. It is also extremely helpful to add a Vitamin B supplement to the wine must in order to assist the yeast. This can be done by dissolving two or three vitamin B_1 tablets in a wine must, or by using a vitaminized yeast nutrient such as Tronozymol. Vitamin B_1 tablets are available from winemaking shops or chemists, who sell them under various trade names or under the chemical name of thiamine hydrochloride. Do not use any tablets which have a strong colour and smell — this may be apparent in the finished wine.

Finally, some winemakers feel that they can save money by re-using the yeast sediment left in the fermentation vessel when a wine has been racked. This is a misguided, not to say foolish, action. To save the insignificant price of a new packet of yeast, they are risking the dangers of off-flavours from dead yeast and the spread of infection from one wine to another should it have been accidentally contaminated at any stage.

THE PROCESS OF FERMENTATION

This is an appropriate place at which to consider the mechanism of fermentation in more detail.

Under well oxygenated conditions, yeast reproduces rapidly and uses available sugar to produce energy by a process of aerobic metabolism. The by-products of this metabolism are carbon dioxide and water:

$$C_6 H_{12} O_6 \quad + \quad 6 O_2 \quad \rightarrow \quad 6 CO_2 \quad + \quad 6 H_2O$$

Sugar   Oxgyen   Carbon dioxide   Water

This process begins in the starter bottle, and continues during the pulp fermentation. It tails off completely when the wine is put under air-lock in the demijohn. At the same time, as the carbon dioxide gas builds up, the yeast gradually switches to anaerobic metabolism, the by-products of which are carbon dioxide and alcohol:

$$C_6 H_{12} O_6 \quad \rightarrow 2 C_2 H_5 OH + \quad 2 CO_2$$

Sugar   Alcohol   Carbon dioxide

This is the source of the alcohol in the wine. The production of a certain amount of alcohol during the pulp fermentation leaches out the flavour and colour of the winemaking ingredients. But the major part of the conversion of sugar to alcohol occurs in the demijohn where air is excluded.

Like all living organisms, yeast has an optimum temperature range. It is killed at temperatures over 35°C (95°F) and works extremely slowly below 15°C (59°F). The exact temperature during fermentation is not critical; an ideal range seems to be 20°–25°C (68°–77°F).

In fact it is probably more important to avoid fluctuations in temperature than to keep exactly to those figures. Fluctuations have a very disruptive effect on the smooth progress of a fermentation. Therefore in cold weather it may be useful to build some kind of fermentation cabinet, well insulated and heated by a low-power electric light bulb. Alternatively, the floor or a shelf near a radiator and out of cold draughts, or an airing cupboard, may provide a suitable and fairly constant temperature. If you wish to be really sophisticated, three types of demijohn heaters are commercially available: (a) an electrically heated mat on which the fermentation vessel stands; (b) an electrically heated belt which wraps around the vessel; and (c) a thermostatically-controlled immersion heater which fits through the demijohn bung.

Fermentation generally lasts from one to five months from the time when the wine is transferred to a demijohn. This wide range of time depends on many factors: the availability of nutrient to the yeast, the amount of sugar in the wine and the temperature being the most obvious. In an extremely hot, dry summer, fermentation may proceed to completion in as little as two weeks. (Don't mistake this situation for a "stuck" fermentation, which is one where the yeast has stopped working for some reason while there is only a little alcohol and a lot of sugar in the wine. This is described in more detail in the section "Faults and remedies", page 89.)

CONCENTRATED GRAPE JUICE

As I mentioned earlier, concentrated grape juice is ideal for making into wine in its own right. These concentrates are now of high quality and produce good results, but they do not present so much of a challenge to the home winemaker as do country wines. However, that is not the main point here. Rather, my emphasis is on the use of concentrated grape juice as an additive to country wine.

Any finished wine, no matter what the ingredients, should have that quality known as *vinosity* or *vinousness*. That is to say it should have those characteristics which make grape wines so distinctive: aroma, body, and the way it tastes in the mouth before and after swallowing. Clearly the most obvious way of mirroring these qualities in a finished wine is to include some grape juice in a must, the "usual" quantity being 9 oz (250 g); both red and white concentrated grape juices are available in this size of container. However, it is far more economical to buy a large can and use it as required — the concentrate will keep in a refrigerator if it is transferred to a sterile glass jar and sealed tightly once the can has been opened. (For safety's sake, it is better not to store half-empty cans.)

Some recipes call for up to one pint (600 ml) of concentrated grape juice — notably flower wines, where the flower petals alone contribute nothing but bouquet and flavour to a wine. On the other hand, some recipes do not need any grape juice, the ingredients themselves being able to produce a balanced must and a high quality, vinous drink.

Bananas are one fruit able to impart body to a wine, and they are frequently used as a substitute or addition to grape juice. Their own flavour, however, is rather pronounced. This can be reduced by discarding the skins, chopping the fruit into water and boiling for about fifteen minutes, during which time the pungent chemicals responsible for the strong banana flavour are driven off. The body which the resulting liquor provides in a finished wine is due to the presence of unfermentable compounds in solution — chiefly glycerol-like molecules, which can link weakly together and give a viscous appearance. Such compounds may actually be produced by the yeast during fermentation. This is said to be one characteristic of the Sauternes yeast strain, and the great body of Sauternes wine is certainly one of the wine's most notable features.

Raisins or sultanas were the old-fashioned substitute for concentrated grape juice, and they are still useful and very suitable. One problem now, perhaps, is that they are rather expensive. One pound (450 g) of raisins or sultanas substitutes for one pint (600 ml) of concentrated grape juice. Note, however, that the high sugar content of concentrated grape juice means less granulated sugar need be added to a must. The appropriate amounts are indicated in each recipe.

Although many winemakers insist on the addition of grape juice to all their wines, I would not be so dogmatic. It can and does help to produce better wines, yet there are many recipe books which make no mention of it at all. I have included it in the recipes wherever I believe it has some useful contribution to make.

The different varieties of concentrated grape juice are discussed fully on pages 94-6.

SUGAR

Once you develop an enthusiasm for winemaking, you may wish to experiment with recipes from all sorts of odd places. You may then discover old recipes which specify candy sugar, treacle, syrup, loaf sugar and so on. New recipes, on the other hand, specify granulated sugar, honey, sucrose, glucose and fructose. This diversity of names is far less confusing than it seems.

First of all, forget all the old recipes. They originated in the days when pure sugar was not easily obtained. In any case, treacle, golden syrup and brown sugar are best avoided, because they impart to a wine distinctive flavours which may conflict with the flavour of the basic ingredients. Honey is used only in mead recipes.

Secondly, in all modern recipes, pure, cheap, granulated white sugar is by far the easiest and best sort of sugar to use. (Incidentally, no matter what you might think or believe, cane and beet sugar are identical. Their chemical name is *sucrose*.)

Thirdly, don't be confused by names, such as sucrose, glucose, fructose and lactose. Sucrose is the chemical name of ordinary white sugar. Sucrose is said to be a "two-unit" sugar because each molecule of sucrose is made up of one glucose and one fructose molecule joined together. Thus it follows that glucose and fructose are simple "one-unit" sugars. Yeast begins its fermentation of sucrose by splitting sucrose into glucose and fructose:

$$C_{12} H_{22} O_{11} + H_2O \rightarrow C_6 H_{12} O_6 + C_6 H_{12} O_6$$

| Sucrose | Water | Glucose | Fructose |

50

The glucose and fructose are then fermented by the yeast in the way described earlier. (You will see that glucose and fructose have the same chemical formula; they differ in the shape of the overall molecule.)

It has been claimed that yeast can be helped, as it were, by the winemaker if he or she supplies the sugar already split into glucose and fructose, i.e. "inverted". This is actually open to question, but if you wish to try it yourself, do not not buy glucose (which is expensive), but invert the amount of white sugar specified in the recipe by boiling it in water with a teaspoonful of citric acid for ten minutes. The syrup should be allowed to cool and then used in the preparation of the must; it will have a pale yellow colour. The acid is not affected by the boiling and therefore takes the place of the same amount of acid in the recipe.

Lactose is another two-unit sugar, but with one important difference to sucrose: it cannot be fermented by yeast. This is because yeast does not produce the enzyme necessary to digest lactose. As far as the winemaker is concerned, the important point is that lactose can be used to sweeten a finished wine without any danger of the yeast restarting fermentation. This is discussed more fully on pages 67-8.

Although yeast lives off sugar in the must, it is inhibited or killed if the sugar is present at too high a concentration. Thus the ideal winemaking practice is to add the sugar in stages: for example, a proportion of the sugar is added at the start of pulp fermentation and the remainder when the wine is transferred to demijohn. In the making of strong wines which require over 3 lb (1.35 kg) of sugar in each gallon (4.5 litres), the sugar is added in even smaller doses — a technique which helps the yeast to achieve very high levels of alcohol.*

But whether the sugar is added in stages or all at once, it must be completely dissolved and well mixed into the wine. Otherwise it will sink to the bottom and form a syrupy layer on the yeast sediment; the yeast will then without doubt be killed. There are

* A table showing the relationship between the weight of sugar in one gallon (4.5 litres) of must and the % alcohol formed during fermentation can be found on page 60.

two ways of avoiding this. First, the fermenting wine can be poured onto the sugar in a sterile basin and stirred well until it is dissolved (but without heating the wine, for that would also kill the yeast). Secondly, the sugar may be added as a syrup. The so-called "standard" syrup is made by dissolving 2 lb of sugar in 1 pint of boiling water. This produces a total volume of 2 pints of syrup. Thus the addition of 1 pint of this syrup to the wine will effectively add 1 lb of sugar in a form which can easily be mixed into the bulk. However, to reiterate the point, it is important that this mixing be done thoroughly, or the dense syrup will simply sink to the bottom of the fermentation vessel and kill the yeast.

Always remember that there is an increase in volume when sugar dissolves in a liquid. (*In British non-metric units*, dissolved sugar occupies a volume in pints equal to exactly half the weight in pounds. For example, 2 lb of sugar dissolved in a must occupies 1 pint in volume; ½ lb of sugar occupies ¼ pint in volume. *In metric units*, the relationship is not so convenient: 1 kg of sugar increases the volume of the liquid in which it is dissolved by about 630 ml.) Whether you add the sugar in stages or all at once, remember to allow for this increase in volume. Final topping-up can be done when any foaming has died away and all the sugar has been added.

THE TYPE OF WINE:

Dry, medium or sweet?
Aperitif, table, social or dessert wine?

Clearly the weight of sugar dissolved in a must determines the final amount of alcohol produced — but only up to the limit of the yeast's tolerance of alcohol. Over about 14%–17% alcohol the yeast stops working and any remaining sugar stays unconverted, thereby producing a sweet wine. Now, each pound (450 g) of sugar in one gallon (4.5 litres) of must will produce about 5% alcohol by volume. One can make use of this fact to construct a rough-and-ready guide to the type of wine which will be produced, according to the overall amount of sugar in each gallon (4.5 litres) of must:

About 2¼ lb (1 kg) — Dry
About 2½ lb (1.15 kg) — Medium
Over 2½ lb (1.15 kg) — Sweet

(Allowing for the smaller US gallon, the corresponding figures for American readers are: about 1¾ lb — Dry; about 2¼ lb — Medium; over 2¼ lb — Sweet.)

I am sure it is obvious just how unsatisfactory this method is: for one thing, the extent to which yeast ferments out the sugar in a wine depends on many very variable factors such as temperature, nutrient and the length of the pulp fermentation.

Clearly it is better to use enough sugar to produce a wine of the desired strength and then to sweeten the finished wine to taste after it has been racked and stabilized. (This is discussed in detail on page 66.) In fact the appropriate level of alcohol in a finished wine depends on what you are aiming to do with it.

Here is a list of definitions of various types of wine:

Aperitif A wine drunk before a meal to stimulate the appetite.

Table wine A wine drunk during a meal. Medium-strength bouquet and flavour, usually dryish with rather less body than a social or a dessert wine. 10%–12% alcohol by volume.

Social wine The name is self-explanatory, really. Intended for drinking at any time other than before, during or after a meal. Has a heavier body and stronger bouquet and flavour than a table wine; usually also sweeter and stronger than a table wine.

Dessert wine Drunk with and after the sweet or dessert course of a meal. Has a stronger flavour and heavier body than either a table or a social wine. Also needs a high level of alcohol to "carry" its sweetness. Quite unsuitable for use during the main courses of a meal.

To illustrate this in more detail, here for comparison are the approximate alcohol contents of some commercial (i.e. grape) wines:

German white table wines (Hock, Liebfraumilch)	8%–11%
(Moselle)	9%
French white table wines (Bordeaux)	11.5%
French red table wines (Bordeaux)	11.5%
(Burgundy)	12.0%
Italian red table wine (Chianti)	11.5%–13%
French white dessert wine (Sauternes)	14%–15%
Champagne or sparkling white wine	8%–10%
Vermouth	14.5%–17.5%
Sherry	17%
Port	17%

These figures suggest that a good target for an average home-made wine would be 13%–14% alcohol by volume. This would allow for a slight dilution when the wine was racked (see page 63), and eventually produce a drink suitable for use as an aperitif or as a table wine — depending on the nature of the ingredients — and perhaps also, with a little judicious sweetening, as a social wine.

PRODUCING STRONGER WINES

The traditional dessert wine is strong, sweet and full-bodied. Something like a commercially produced dessert wine can be made at home by aiming for a high alcoholic content and good body. The alcohol level is achieved by adding the sugar in stages: half the total amount at the beginning and the remainder in 4-ounce (110g) lots each time the previous lot of sugar has been almost fermented away. This can be judged by watching the progress of bubbles through the air-lock or by tasting the wine, although the use of a hydrometer is more reliable and makes things easier (page 56). Once the correct strength has been achieved, the wine can be stabilized, racked and finally sweetened to taste. The amount of sugar required to do this is discussed on page 66.

The good body of a dessert wine is achieved by the use of more fruit than in a table wine. Equally, these wines need more acid to balance high levels of sugar and prevent a cloying sickly sweet taste when the wine is drunk. If in doubt, use ½ oz (15 g) of tartaric acid per gallon (4.5 litres) — any excess will precipitate out — and up to the equivalent of 6–7 lb (2.7–3.2 kg) of fruit as opposed to the more normal 3–4 lb (1.35–1.8 kg) of a table wine.

There seems little point in making a strong dry wine at home. One has to drink less — if one wishes to stay sober! — than one would of a table wine, and so the opportunity to enjoy the flavour of the wine to the full is reduced. But one of the enjoyable aspects of this hobby is the fact that you are not tied down to a set of rules. There is no particular reason why one should feel compelled to emulate commercial wines. The method of production is the same as that of strong sweet wines, except that the final addition of sugar is allowed to ferment to dryness and the wine is not sweetened to taste.

We should not leave the subject of strong wines without mentioning port and sherry. Although the home winemaker can produce a reasonable "sherry", given a certain amount of care, sadly he cannot really emulate port. This is because of the strange way it is made. Commercially, port is produced by allowing a sweet red wine must to ferment only about a quarter of the way to completion, at which point a considerable amount of brandy is added to stop the fermentation and increase the alcoholic strength to the desired level. The nearest we can realistically come to this process is to sweeten a strong red wine and then to fortify it with a small amount of brandy. Any of the recipes for red dessert wine would be suitable, and the calculations needed for fortifying the wine are explained in a later section.

THE HYDROMETER AND ITS USES IN WINEMAKING

You may be told, or read, that it is impossible to make wine without a hydrometer. That is nonsense! You could, in fact, go right ahead and make wine without ever using the instrument. Sooner or later, though, you may move on to more advanced winemaking techniques, and a hydrometer can then be useful, for example if you are compiling your own recipes. Or you may wish to add a little sophistication and scientific technique once you have grasped the basic methods.

The hydrometer is made up of a glass tube with a bulb at one end and a graduated scale in the stem (Fig. 3). When placed in a liquid, it floats with the stem protruding out of the liquid surface. The specific gravity (S.G.) of the liquid can then be read off the scale. But what does this mean?

The S.G. of a liquid is in fact a measure of its "thickness" or density; pure water weighs one gram per cubic centimetre, so its S.G. is said to be 1.000. But as you dissolve sugar in water, the water, or rather the sugar solution, becomes thicker: it now has a density greater than that of pure water, so the S.G. will be greater than 1.000. Thus a hydrometer placed in sugar solution will float with the scale showing more than 1.000 at the liquid surface. The S.G. of a wine can be measured in exactly the same way, and the S.G. can then be used to determine the amount of sugar present in the must. This is done by reference to Table 1. The table also shows the per cent of alcohol by volume which is produced for a given weight of sugar in a must, *provided that* the yeast ferments *all* the sugar to alcohol. This figure is shown in the "potential alcohol" column.

The instructions for using a hydrometer are always included with it when you buy it. They need not, therefore, be repeated in full here. To summarize:

1) The hydrometer must be spun when it is floating in the liquid and before taking the reading to dispel any air bubbles which are clinging to the sides of the glass — otherwise they would add extra buoyancy to the hydrometer and produce a false reading.

Fig 3: The hydrometer in action

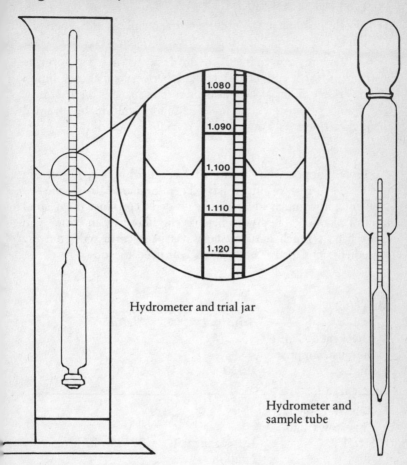

Hydrometer and trial jar

Hydrometer and sample tube

Above: The hydrometer should float freely in the liquid in the trial jar. Inset is an exaggerated illustration of how to read the hydrometer. The scale measurement is taken at the bottom of the meniscus, not where it touches the tube. Here the correct reading is 1.100, *not* 1.096.

Right: This device can simplify the measurement of specific gravity. The glass container fits into the mouth of a demijohn, and a sample of wine can be drawn up by squeezing the rubber bulb. The hydrometer then floats in the sample of wine.

2) The hydrometer must be floating freely, away from the sides of the jar or trial tube.

3) Take the reading at the bottom of the meniscus, not where the liquid actually touches the hydrometer stem (Fig. 3).

It is fair to say that the hydrometer is not an accurate instrument, for it cannot differentiate between sugar in solution and any other material such as fruit pulp in suspension in a must. The liquid or must being tested should therefore be strained through a fine mesh sieve before its S.G. is determined.

Example: Suppose that a wine of 15% alcohol is required. Six pints (3.4 litres) of must have been prepared from the ingredients; how much sugar will be needed to produce the desired level of alcohol? The hydrometer is the only way in which you can tell how much natural sugar has been extracted from the ingredients and hence how much you need to add.

METHOD:

	British	*Metric*
1 Check the S.G. of the must. Suppose this is:	1.030	1.030
2 Refer to Table 1. This shows that S.G. 1.030 =	13¼ oz sugar in 1 gallon	376 g in 4.5 litres
3 Adjust this figure to give the weight of sugar in 6 pints (3.4 litres) of must =	$\frac{6}{8} \times 13\frac{1}{4} = 10$ oz	$\frac{3.4}{4.5} \times 376 = 284$ g

4 Refer to Table 1. Check the weight of sugar required for a wine of 15% (14.9%) alcohol =	2 lb 15 oz per gallon	1332 g per 4.5 litres

5 Subtract weight of sugar already present in must to determine the amount to be added =	2 lb 5 oz	1048 g

Note: Most of the recipes in this book refer to 1 gallon (4.5 litres) of wine. However, a demijohn actually holds 8½ pints (4.8 litres) up to the base of the neck. This can produce a slightly weaker wine than the figures indicate for a given amount of sugar. Generally the error is insignificant; but if you want to be really precise, you can add an extra 1 oz (28 g) of sugar for each 1 lb (450 g) specified in Table 1 overleaf.

"GRAVITY" AND SPECIFIC GRAVITY

Some authors talk in terms of gravity rather than specific gravity. In fact gravity refers to nothing more than those figures of the specific gravity which fall after the decimal point. Thus, for example, S.G. 1.020 becomes gravity 20; S.G. 1.115 becomes gravity 115. For specific gravities less than 1.000, the gravity becomes negative: for example, S.G. 0.995 equals gravity − 5.

CONTROLLING THE SUGAR

I have already mentioned that yeast is unable to work efficiently

TABLE 1
HYDROMETER CHART
(The corresponding table for US readers is shown in Appendix II, page 183)

Specific gravity	Amount of sugar in*		4.5 litres grams	Potential alcohol (% by volume)
	1 gallon			
	lb	oz		
1.010		4¾	135	0.4
1.015		7	198	1.2
1.020		9	255	2.0
1.025		11½	326	2.8
1.030		13¼	376	3.6
1.035		15½	439	4.3
1.040	1	1½	496	5.1
1.045	1	3½	553	5.8
1.050	1	5½	610	6.5
1.055	1	7¾	673	7.2
1.060	1	9¾	730	7.9
1.065	1	11¾	787	8.6
1.070	1	14	851	9.3
1.075	2	0	907	10.0
1.080	2	2½	978	10.6
1.085	2	4½	1035	11.3
1.090	2	6½	1091	12.0
1.095	2	8¾	1155	12.7
1.100	2	10¾	1212	13.4
1.105	2	12¾	1269	14.2
1.110	2	15	1332	14.9
1.115	3	1	1389	15.6
1.120	3	3¼	1453	16.3
1.125	3	5¼	1510	17.1
1.130	3	7½	1573	17.8
1.135	3	9½	1630	18.5
1.140	3	11¾	1694	19.3

*Remember that these figures refer to the amount of sugar dissolved in a must to give a total volume of one gallon or 4.5 litres. They do *not* refer to the amount of sugar *added* to one gallon (4.5 litres) of liquid.

This information is reproduced from Boots product literature, by kind permission of The Boots Company PLC.

if too much sugar is dissolved in a must. If you have a hydrometer, aim not to exceed S.G. 1.100 at any time. Any extra sugar is best added when the conversion of sugar to alcohol during fermentation has reduced the S.G. to 1.010 or less.

CHECKING THE PROGRESS OF FERMENTATION; PRODUCING STRONG WINES

While a wine is fermenting, samples of the wine may be extracted at intervals and the S.G. determined. As the fermentation proceeds, the sugar is fermented to alcohol and the S.G. falls. The rate of fall decreases as fermentation nears completion; and when no change in readings occurs over a period of two or three weeks, the ferment will have ended.

The hydrometer is especially useful in producing strong wines. When producing a strong and sweet wine, it is best to add half the sugar at the start of fermentation and the remainder in 4-oz (110 g) lots each time the S.G. falls to 1.010 or less. This will avoid producing an over-sweet wine. If, however, you want a strong, dry wine, allow the S.G. to fall to 1.000 before each addition of sugar, and add it in 2-oz (55 g) lots when nearing the point at which the yeast cannot work because of the high level of alcohol.

WHEN FERMENTATION IS COMPLETE

As I suggested earlier, the ideal winemaking practice is to ferment a wine to dryness at the desired level of alcohol and then sweeten to taste. Clearly sugar cannot be added until the wine is perfectly clear and all traces of yeast have been removed from it, otherwise fermentation will restart. (This does not apply if the unfermentable sugar lactose is used.)

When a wine has fermented to dryness, those yeast cells which have been in suspension will fall to the bottom and add to the sediment or "lees". As the sediment thickens, the wine will begin to clear noticeably. This is the time to rack, i.e. to siphon the wine off the yeast sediment.

Occasionally one sees books which recommend racking as soon as one month after the wine has been placed in the demijohn — whether or not the fermentation is complete. This is bad winemaking practice. The bulk of the yeast colony forms a light sediment on the bottom of the fermentation vessel soon after it has been set up, and racking before the fermentation has ended will clearly leave only those yeast cells in suspension in the wine. This could deplete the colony to a point where it would almost certainly be inadequate to carry fermentation through to completion. So why do some books recommend such early racking? The answer seems to be that if fruit pulp and debris have passed into the demijohn, they may impart unpleasant flavours if they are left in the wine; hence the need for early racking. In my view, however, this problem should not arise if the pulp has been strained correctly. Therefore in general, once a fermenting must has been put under air-lock, it should remain there until the fermentation has finished.

The simplest way to tell when fermentation is complete is to see whether any bubbles are rising to the surface of the wine or passing through the air-lock. Other useful ways to judge the point at which to rack include —

- *The change in appearance of a wine:* Although a wine will not be completely clear, a *firm* sediment will have formed and it will look less murky than it did when it was fermenting vigorously.

- *The taste of the wine:* There should be a high level of alcohol and little, if any, sweetness.

- *The rate of fall of the specific gravity*, if you are using a hydrometer, as explained on page 56.

RACKING

The formation of a good firm sediment can be encouraged by moving the wine into a cool place. However, if the wine has finished fermenting, a sediment should form quickly of its own accord. In any event, once the wine has cleared significantly, *and you are sure the fermentation is over* — rack!

Racking is simplicity itself. The jar containing yeast and sediment should have been allowed to settle, and be positioned about two feet (60 cm) above a clean, sterile jar of the same size. The air-lock and bung are removed from the top jar and a sterile plastic tube inserted into the wine. Sucking on the open end of the tube (or the careful use of a small siphon pump) causes the tube to fill up. This end of the tube is then placed into the mouth of the lower jar and the wine allowed to flow in, while care is taken to ensure that the upper end of the tube does not disturb the sediment. It is helpful to have a small tap on the lower end of the tube to control the rate of flow when the level of wine in the upper jar nears the sediment: the slower the rate of flow, the less likely that any sediment will be sucked up. Most of the wine in the upper jar can be safely siphoned off the sediment by carefully tilting the jar as the liquid level nears the bottom. The process is illustrated in Figure 4.

The lower jar should now be topped up: see the note on "Topping up and racking" below. Also at this stage, a Campden tablet should be dissolved in each gallon (4.5 litres) of wine to ensure that it keeps well. Any remaining yeast and other suspended matter will drop out of suspension fairly quickly, and a second racking should take place as soon as the wine has cleared completely.

There is no reason why more rackings cannot be carried out if this seems essential; however, with a properly prepared must and careful straining, two rackings are generally enough. Remember that each time the wine is racked it is exposed to the air, with an inevitable danger of infection and oxidation. Although some authors suggest that this can be reduced by adding one Campden tablet at each racking, I do not recommend the

Fig 4A: Racking
Diagram illustrating the stages at which
to rack, or siphon the wine off the sediment.

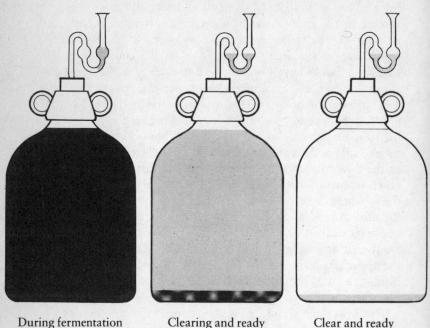

During fermentation   Clearing and ready   Clear and ready
                      for first racking   for second racking

addition of more than a maximum of two per gallon (4.5 litres).
Leaving aside the question of safety for the drinker, the sulphur
dioxide may adversely affect the flavour and colour of the wine.

TOPPING UP AND RACKING

Each time the wine is siphoned off the sediment, a small volume
of liquid will be left in the upper jar. This will obviously produce
an air-space in the lower demijohn. It is important that this jar
be topped up with cool boiled water to the base of the neck: a

Fig 4B: Racking

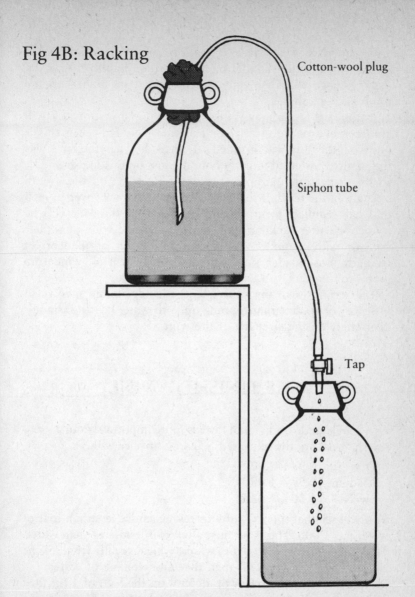

Cotton-wool plug

Siphon tube

Tap

Note that during racking the siphon tube is kept well clear of sediment in the upper jar. As the level of wine nears the bottom of the jar, the danger of sucking sediment into the siphon tube can be reduced by decreasing the flow rate with the small tap. See text for more details.

large air-space may cause oxidation, and this can ruin the flavour of a wine. (Oxidation is explained in the section on storage, page 81.) The only exception to this rule is in the production of sherry.

At first sight, you may think that topping up with water will considerably reduce the strength of the wine. However, this is not so. If the pulp was strained off correctly when the wine was originally transferred to demijohn, the loss on racking should be so small that topping up has a negligible effect on the overall strength of the wine. If for any reason a very thick (over ½ inch or 1 cm) sediment forms during fermentation, the wine may be topped up after racking with another finished wine of similar type or with a mixture of vodka and water at the correct strength. A useful idea may be to make up a "neutral" wine from grape concentrate and use this for topping up.

The second (and any subsequent) racking should involve so little loss of volume that topping up with water has an insignificant effect on the strength of the wine.

THE FINISHED WINE

As a rough guide (individual taste is more important than a set of rules), these are the expected S.G.s of finished wines:

Dry   0.980–1.000
Medium   0.995–1.005
Sweet   1.005–1.020

You will see that the S.G. of a dry wine can be less than that of water, i.e. 1.000. This is because alcohol is less dense than water. Thus a mixture of alcohol and water (which is really what a wine is) will have a lower S.G. than the same volume of water.

Note also that the effect of alcohol on the S.G. of a finished wine makes it impossible to calculate the weight of sugar in a finished wine by measuring its S.G. and referring to Table 1.

If you wish to sweeten a dry wine to taste, you may find the following table helpful.

TABLE 2
AMOUNT OF SWEETENING REQUIRED
IN FINISHED WINES

Type of wine		Weight in oz (grams) of granulated white sugar, i.e. sucrose, required			
		per bottle*		per gallon/4.5 litres	
Table	Medium dry	⅛	(3)	¾	(18)
	Medium sweet	½	(14)	3	(84)
	Sweet	1¼	(35)	7½	(210)
Aperitif	Medium dry	¼	(7)	1½	(42)
	Medium sweet	¾	(21)	4½	(126)
	Sweet	1½	(42)	9	(252)
Social	Medium dry	⅜	(11)	2¼	(66)
	Medium sweet	1	(28)	6	(168)
	Sweet	1¾	(49)	10½	(294)
Dessert	Medium dry	½	(14)	3	(84)
	Medium sweet	1¼	(35)	7½	(210)
	Sweet	2	(56)	12	(336)

* Refers to standard 70 cl (1¼ pint) bottle.
This information is reproduced from the article "More About Sugar" by T. Edwin Belt, which appeared in the April 1983 issue of *Winemaker* magazine, by kind permission of Argus Specialist Publications Limited.

These figures are a useful guide if you are sweetening a dry wine to taste. However, it is important to remember that they are *only* a guide, and that as your palate becomes more discriminating you will be able to detect smaller amounts of sugar.

As I have already explained, the unfermentable sugar lactose may be used as a sweetening agent without any risk of re-fermentation; however, it is only about one-third as sweet as sucrose, so proportionately more needs to be added. Obviously lactose may be added at any stage of production, whereas sucrose must be added when the wine is perfectly clear and stable.

Saccharin is sometimes suggested as a sweetening agent. One tablet is approximately equal to ⅛ oz (3½ g) of sucrose.

When you are sweetening a finished wine, dissolve the sugar in a little of the wine and add the solution to the bulk a little at a time, mixing well after each addition, until you have achieved a result which suits your palate.

Incidentally, a "dry wine" may not be completely dry; in fact, totally sugar-free wines are often very harsh. A very small amount of sugar in a wine will not necessarily register as "sweetness" on tasting, but will smooth out the flavour and produce a much more pleasant drink.

FINING

If a must is correctly prepared, the wine should clear quickly of its own accord after fermentation. But sometimes a wine stubbornly refuses to clear — even after many months in storage. It may then be "fined". The use of wine finings precipitates out any suspended solids and leaves a clear wine. The only two types which need concern the modern winemaker are isinglass, a protein substance, and bentonite, a powdered clay.

Isinglass is a thick, liquid, proteinaceous substance which is creamed into a little of the wine and then stirred into the bulk. Full instructions will be provided when the substance is purchased — it is available under various brand names such as *Winefine* and *Wine finings* — but the usual amount is ½ oz (15 g) per gallon (4.5 litres). The protein molecules coagulate with the particles causing a haze and drag them to the bottom of the container, where the whole mass forms a thick sediment. This is a fairly rapid procedure, taking from six hours up to two weeks — the exact time depends on the chemical composition of the wine.

The trouble with isinglass is that it also reacts with the tannin and other elements of the wine itself: too much isinglass will therefore remove body, colour, bite and bouquet from the wine. This is called "over-fining", and it is a very real danger. In addition, some hazes are quite unaffected by the substance. Whenever isinglass has been used to fine a wine, more tannin should be added to taste afterwards to replace that which has been precipitated out by the isinglass.

Bentonite is also an effective fining agent and it has the added advantage that it cannot over-fine a wine. It is usually sold as a sterile, dry powder which must be mixed with water and allowed to form a gel before being mixed into the wine, although sachets of ready prepared gel can now be purchased. Bentonite clears some hazes that isinglass will not touch; but there is no cure for pectin or starch hazes except the appropriate enzyme.

Whether you use isinglass or bentonite, once the wine has cleared and a thick sediment of finings and suspended material has precipitated out, rack the wine into a clean, sterile container.

FILTERING

Filtering is the last resort for clearing a wine. It cannot remove pectin or starch hazes from a wine, and what it can achieve (the rapid removal of microscopic particles from a wine) would probably occur in time anyway.

One situation where filtration may be genuinely useful is when a wine has been prepared for drinking soon after fermentation has ended and the yeast needs to be removed at once. Another use is to "polish" an already clear or bright wine when 100 per cent crystal clarity is required — on special occasions, or when exhibiting, for example.

There is an indefinable loss of quality on filtering, so it is to be avoided if possible. However, if you decide it is necessary, say because a wine simply will not clear, then you have a choice of two methods open to you. The first involves beating a powder into the wine and then passing it through a filter bag. The powder gradually forms a layer on the inner surface of the bag and prevents any particles in the wine passing through. This type of filter is only acceptable if the bag and wine are enclosed in some kind of container which excludes the air. This is illustrated in Figure 5a (overleaf).

The second method is to use a filter kit which siphons the wine

Fig 5A: Filter system using filter powder

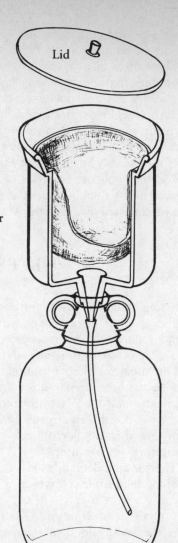

Lid

Plastic filtration container

Filter bag

Receiving demijohn

Outlet tube

In this system, a filter medium (crystals or powder) is mixed with the wine, which is then poured into the filter bag. A layer of powder builds up on the inner surface of the bag and removes any sediment as the wine trickles through.

Fig 5B: Filter system using filter pads

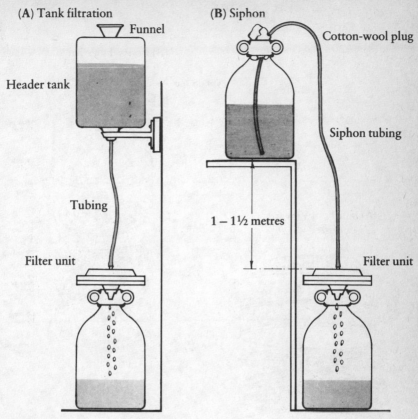

(A) Tank filtration

Funnel

Header tank

Tubing

Filter unit

(B) Siphon

Cotton-wool plug

Siphon tubing

1 – 1½ metres

Filter unit

The diagram illustrates two methods of filtration using a filter kit with pads. The siphon method, shown on the right, is the method usually suggested, and indeed it generally works very well. However, if the fermentation has only recently been completed, the new wine may still contain a large amount of dissolved gas. This gas may be given off during filtering and can collect in the bend of the siphon tube, slowing down or even stopping the filtration process. Obviously this can be an aggravating problem if one is filtering several gallons of wine. The problem can be overcome though by using a tank filtration kit (available from Southern Vinyards of Hove, East Sussex). As the diagram on the left shows, there is a straight drop from the header tank to the filter unit; this allows any gas given off to escape upwards into the tank, thus avoiding any "air-locks" in the system.

Fig 5C: Diagram showing internal structure of filter systems

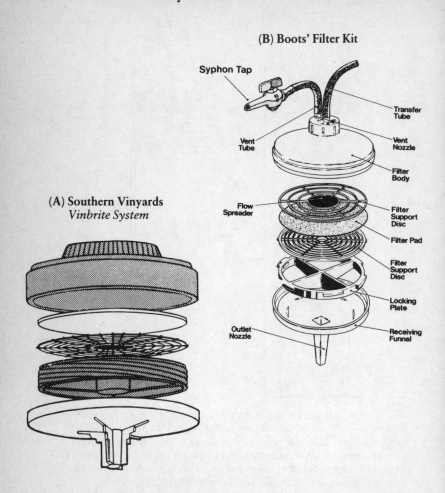

(B) Boots' Filter Kit

Syphon Tap

Transfer Tube

Vent Tube

Vent Nozzle

Filter Body

(A) Southern Vinyards
Vinbrite System

Flow Spreader

Filter Support Disc

Filter Pad

Filter Support Disc

Locking Plate

Outlet Nozzle

Receiving Funnel

In both cases, the filter pad is the crucial part of the filter which removes sediment and haze from the wine. Similar systems are marketed by a number of other companies. *(With thanks to Southern Vinyards Ltd and The Boots Company Plc.)*

Fig 5D: Pressure filter
kit using filter pads

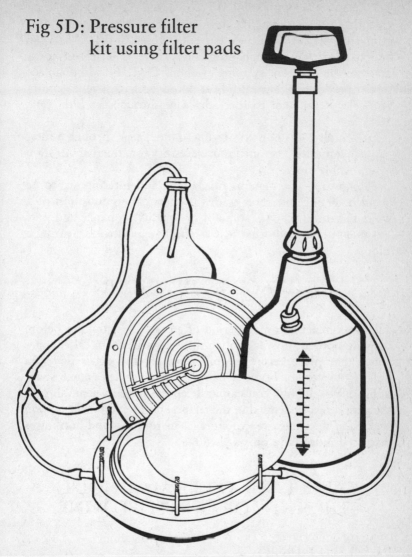

This unit, although rather expensive at around £27.50, is a boon to anyone who makes wine regularly or in large quantities. Using the pressure pump shown, it will speedily clear even the murkiest wines! *(Available from Johnson Home Wine Supplies Ltd, 12 The Hornet, Chichester, Sussex PO19 4JG. It is called the Vinamat.)*

through a fine filter pad or layer of filter powders built up on a porous plastic sheet. The wine is not exposed to the air and can be left to trickle through gradually. There is little to choose between the different systems available (Fig. 5b), although for sheer speed, it is hard to beat those which have a pump-pressurized container to force the wine through the filter (Fig. 5c).

Incidentally, it is hopeless trying to filter wine through a filter paper in a funnel. The fine grade necessary for effective filtration is impossibly slow.

To sum up: as a general rule, fining and filtering are to be avoided. Fining interferes with the chemical composition of a wine, filtration removes some of the quality. Patience and time are much better and often just as effective agents for clearing a wine!

STORAGE IN DEMIJOHN

All wines benefit from a period of storage in demijohn before they are bottled. It is as though the necessary chemical changes which take place before a wine is mature can occur better in bulk. However, the home winemaker may not have much space at his disposal. So if you cannot keep the wine in demijohn for the period recommended in the recipes, bottle it after the *second* racking. The whole area of storage, maturation and bottling is discussed more fully on pages 80–6.

CALCULATING THE ALCOHOLIC STRENGTH OF A FINISHED WINE

BY GRAVITY DROP

The first step in calculating the alcoholic strength of a finished wine is to subtract the final S.G. of the wine from the initial S.G. of the must after all the sugar has been added and the liquid made up to its full volume.

Example:

Initial S.G.	1110 (omit the decimal point)
Final S.G.	995
Drop in gravity	115

Next, the figure obtained in this way is divided by 7.4. The result obtained is the % alcohol by volume in the wine, i.e. 115 ÷ 7.4 = 15.5% alcohol. Although this method is unlikely to be accurate to within ½%, it is a good approximation.

Problems arise, of course, if you have added the sugar in stages, because the volume of the wine changes after each addition. The % alcohol can then only be calculated by determining the sum of all the drops in gravity between the various additions of sugar and adjusting for the changes in the volume of the wine. However, this is a tedious and inaccurate procedure. In such a case it is much more realistic simply to add up the total weight of sugar added to the wine and use Table 1 to determine the potential % of alcohol. This should correspond to the % alcohol in the finished wine — provided that it is dry, i.e. that all the sugar has been fermented to alcohol. If the fermentation was stopped while the wine was still sweet, or if sugar has been added before the final S.G. was determined, the following method is the one to use.

BY EVAPORATION

This method relies on the fact that alcohol evaporates at a temperature well below the boiling point of water. So when a wine is heated, the alcohol evaporates, and as it does so, the S.G. of the wine increases. This method has the advantage that one does not need to know the initial S.G. of the must.

Method:

1. The wine's final S.G. is measured.

2. A sample of wine is then transferred to a bottle of about ½ pint (300 ml) capacity — the volume is not critical — and the level of wine is adjusted exactly to a mark on the narrowest part of the neck.

3. The wine is then poured into a pan (or preferably a conical flask) and boiled for five minutes so that the alcohol is driven

off. The loss of spray droplets should be minimized, so boil *gently*.

4. The liquid is then allowed to cool, transferred back to the measuring bottle and topped up with water exactly to the measurement mark, so that its volume before and after boiling is the same — but without the alcohol.

5. The S.G. is measured once again. The first reading is subtracted from the second and the alcohol level obtained by reference to Table 3.

Example:

S.G. after boiling	1.019
S.G. before boiling	1.003
Increase in S.G.	0.016

Refer to Table 3:
0.016 = 12.3% alcohol.

Note: Although the actual temperature at which the S.G. is measured is not critical, the first and second readings of the S.G. must be taken at the *same* temperature.

% ALCOHOL AND DEGREES PROOF

Although the accepted modern method of expressing the alcoholic content of drinks is the % alcohol by volume, one often still sees references to "degrees (°) proof". The conversion between these two systems is simple:

To convert from % alcohol to ° proof
  Multiply by 7, divide by 4
  Example: 15% alcohol = $\dfrac{15 \times 7}{4}$ = 26.25°

To convert from ° proof to % alcohol
  Multiply by 4, divide by 7
  Example: 70° proof = $\dfrac{70 \times 4}{7}$ = 40% alcohol

Standard spirits — whisky, vodka and so on — are 70° proof, or 40% alcohol by volume.

TABLE 3
Calculation of Strength of Wine from Increase in S.G. on Boiling

Increase in S.G.	% alcohol by volume
.008	5.7
.009	6.4
.010	7.2
.011	8.1
.012	8.8
.013	9.7
.014	10.6
.015	11.4
.016	12.3
.017	13.2
.018	14.1
.019	15.1
.020	16.0
:021	17.0
.022	18.0
.023	19.0
.024	20.0
.025	21.0

FORTIFICATION: INCREASING THE ALCOHOLIC STRENGTH

Unless you are experienced, it is difficult to judge accurately the alcoholic strength of a finished wine. Don't, therefore, assume that your wine is weak without first tasting a commercial wine of similar type. However, if your wine *is* low in alcohol, or if you wish to use the wine as a dessert wine or as "port" or "sherry", you may want to add either a stronger wine or a spirit to increase its strength. Vodka is ideal for this purpose, of course, since it has no flavour of its own; alternatively, "Polish Spirit", which is twice as strong as vodka, can be used. A word of warning, here, though! The alcohol in beers, wines, spirits and so on is *ethanol* (also known as ethyl alcohol). All other alcohols are very poisonous. You MUST therefore use a reputable supplier or brand of spirits.

The calculation of how much spirit need be added to a wine to increase its strength by a known amount can be simplified by use of the *Pearson Square*, which looks like this:

where A = Strength of spirit to be added

B = Strength of wine at present

C = Required strength of wine after fortification

D = C − B

E = A − C

The proportion of spirit to wine which will give the desired result will then be equal to D/E.

Example:
4.5 litres of wine at 13.2% alcohol by volume are to be fortified to an alcoholic strength of 17% with the use of 70° vodka. How much spirit is required?

Method (1)
- Convert all strengths to same units, here, degrees proof
  13.2% alcohol = 23.1°
  17% alcohol = 29.75°

- Substitute these values as follows:
  A = Strength of spirit to be added = 70°
  B = Strength of wine at present = 23.1°
  C = Strength of wine required = 29.75°
  D = C − B = 29.75 − 23.1 = 6.65
  E = A − C = 70 − 29.75 = 40.25

- The required proportions of spirit and wine are D:E = 6.65:40.25 = 1:6 (approximately). Therefore 4.5 litres of wine would require the addition of one-sixth of that volume of spirit, i.e. 750 ml.

Method (2)
- Using the same example, but substituting the following values:

  4.5 litres = 6 (standard) wine bottles

  70° proof = 40% alcohol

- Then A = Strength of spirit to be added = 40%

    B = Strength of wine at present = 13.2%

    C = Strength of wine required = 17%

    D = C − B = 17 − 13.2 = 3.8

    E = A − C = 40 − 17 = 23.0

- The required proportions of spirit and wine are D:E = 3.8:23.0 = 1:6 (approximately).

  Therefore six bottles of wine would require the addition of one bottle of vodka of the same size.

If you are blending two wines of known strength, or wine and water (e.g. when topping up at racking), and wish to know the strength of the final mixture, the formula is as follows:

$$\text{Strength of mixture} = \frac{(A \times C) + (B \times D)}{A + B}$$

where A = No. of parts of first wine

    B = No. of parts of second wine

    C = Strength of first wine

where D = Strength of second wine

Example:

8 pints of wine of 12.5% alcohol are blended with 4 pints of wine of 15% alcohol. What strength is the blend?

$$\text{Strength} = \frac{(8 \times 12.5) + (4 \times 15)}{8 + 4} = \frac{100 + 60}{12} = \frac{160}{12} = 13.3\%$$

In such calculations, the strength of water is of course entered as 0.

BLENDING WINES

No matter how much care you take, there will always be times when you produce a wine which does not come up to requirements. Of course any wine which is tainted, or infected, or has a peculiar taste or smell should be thrown away. But wines which are basically sound may be blended to improve them. The principle is very, very simple: you aim to blend two faulty wines so that their faults cancel each other out. Thus, for example, an over-acid wine can be blended with a dull, insipid one; an over-astringent wine can be blended with one that lacks bite; one with too much body can be blended with a "thin" one; one that is too sweet can be blended with a dry one; and so on.

The procedure must be carefully controlled: start by blending small samples, and when you have achieved a satisfactory combination, use the same proportions in bulk. The difficulty is that having adjusted one quality, say acidity, by mixing two wines, then another quality, say flavour or sweetness, may no longer be acceptable. You may therefore blend two wines to correct a particular defect, and then mix the blend with another "straight" wine (or even a second blend) to conceal or rectify another fault. However, as you might expect, the best blends are those which consist of two similar wines, each with a single opposing fault.

Once you have blended, the mixture may throw a precipitate or re-ferment. Thus the new wine should be kept in bulk for at least three months before final judgement is passed. The flavour at this point may have changed considerably. If it is acceptable, bottle it; if not, cut your losses and throw it away.

Perhaps it is worth emphasizing that you cannot blend wines with any hope of success unless you are able to identify the different characteristics and defects of wine in the first place.

STORAGE, MATURATION AND BOTTLING

Although hard-and-fast rules about the storage of home-made wine are simply too generalized to be helpful, there is no doubt that almost all wines benefit from at least some storage. (The exceptions include those wines deliberately made to be consumed while they are still young.) So, rather than lay down a set of rules, I shall offer some guidelines for storage:

1 The purpose of storage is to allow the wine to mature, i.e. to allow
   (i) complete merging of different elements in the wine and the round-off of any acidic or sharp edges in the flavour; (ii) the development of a good bouquet by the reaction of acid and alcohol so as to produce esters; (iii) the precipitation of excess tannin and acid (especially in red wines), so that a well balanced, fruity, smooth drink is produced.

2 All wines benefit from a period of storage in bulk before they are bottled, even if this is only the time between the end of fermentation and the second racking.

3 All storage must be done in containers with the minimum air-space. See the note on oxidation below.

4 Red or rosé wines should be stored in dark or shaded jars and green bottles or they will discolour.

5 Generally white wines need less storage than red. Many white wines can be drunk soon after the fermentation is over and nearly all will be ready at six months, although dessert wines may need up to two years in storage.

6 Light red wines will probably be ready anywhere between two and six months after fermentation, but those fermented on the pulp contain more tannin and may need longer storage — up to eighteen months. Dessert wines may need two years or even longer storage before they are at their best.

7 After bottling, a wine needs at least four weeks' storage before it is served, to re-adjust, as it were, to the introduction of oxygen during bottling and its new environment. If you plan to drink it young, adjust your schedule accordingly.

OXIDATION

Oxidation is a chemical change that takes place in a wine in the presence of air. It involves the conversion of alcohol to acetaldehyde. This compound is a vital element of a sherry, but its taste and smell are out of place in a normal wine. Sulphite displaces oxygen from a wine and prevents the conversion; it can also reverse a slight oxidation by reacting with acetaldehyde to produce a colourless, odourless compound.

Thus the addition of one Campden tablet per gallon (4.5 litres) at the first racking acts as a safeguard against oxidation; and another tablet may be added for the same reason when the wine is bottled. But whether or not you have added sulphite, storing wine in a cask or demijohn with an air-space will ruin it. Keep the vessels topped up!

Incidentally, the presence of an air-space over the liquid of a fermenting wine in a container sealed with an air-lock will not be detrimental. This is because the oxygen is displaced by the inert carbon dioxide gas formed during fermentation.

DARKENING

Slight darkening of a wine may be a feature of oxidation or a natural light-induced colour change. It may be reversed by the addition of a little ascorbic acid (vitamin C).

STORAGE IN CASKS

Do not be deluded into thinking that fermenting or maturing your wine in a cask will effect a miraculous improvement in quality! To start with, casks *less* than 6 gallons (30 litres) in capacity are to be avoided as storage vessels since their high surface-area to volume ratio exposes the wine to the danger of oxidation. Some smaller new wood casks are lined with wax, which renders the wood impermeable; but surely one might as well then use glass? A second problem is that second-hand casks are often stripped, scorched and re-assembled before being sold. This renders the wood hard and impermeable. And thirdly, a cask always leaks if it has a tap fitted.

Despite this, casks of over 6 gallons (30 litres) can be useful, particularly for the maturing and mellowing of red wine. If you wish to try using one you should:

1. Wash it out with hot water.

2. Sterilize it for twenty-four hours with a solution of bleach (4 fl oz per gallon or 30 ml per 4.5 litres) and then rinse it well.

3. Check that the wood has swollen and is not leaking; wash it out with 1 gallon (4.5 litres) of wine.

4. Use it for one fermentation to check it is wholesome and then re-sterilize it with metabisulphite before storing wine in it.

5. Lay it on its side when using it for storage, and support both ends and the centre.

6. Check it regularly and top up whenever necessary.

PLASTIC CONTAINERS

Cannot be recommended as the alcohol may evaporate away through the plastic and the wine may in any case be tainted.

STORAGE TEMPERATURES

For the average homewinemaker, with wine stored in any available space, rules about cellarcraft are irrelevant. In fact storage conditions are not really critical, so long as the storage vessels are sterilized before use and sealed with sterilized rubber bungs. (If you use corks in demijohns, the corks must be waxed, since they are otherwise quite porous.) If possible, keep all your storage vessels, including bottles, at an even temperature of between 10°–15°C (50°–60°F).

BOTTLING

All fermentation, blending, sweetening and fortification should have been done before a wine is bottled. The wine will be clear and bright, and the bottles sterilized and rinsed before use. If you have previously added only one Campden tablet per gallon (4.5 litres), another may be added as a safeguard against oxidation before bottling.

The wine is siphoned into (sterile) bottles through a (sterile) siphon tube. A tap on the end of the tube is very useful at this stage since it allows precise control of the flow and prevents spillage when you move from one bottle to another.

BOTTLES . . .

Wines are best in wine bottles — if only for the impressive

presentation which is then possible. However, it would be ridiculous to say that homemade wine "cannot" or "should not" be stored in screw-topped bottles. The important points are these:

1 Second-hand or re-used bottles should be washed with a little detergent and a nylon or plastic bottle brush until they are spotless.

2 They *must* then be rinsed with water until clean.

3 They *must* then be sterilized in one of the normal ways.

4 Red wines should be stored in green or dark bottles to exclude the light, or they will lose their colour.

It is a nice touch to use, if you can, wine bottles of colour and shape which suit the type of wine you are making. Since winemaking shops usually sell only green and colourless glass bottles with straight sides and sharp shoulders, you may have to re-use commercial wine bottles. This is perfectly acceptable, provided they are washed and sterilized before use.

. . . AND STOPPERS

Screw caps are made of metal and plastic. They should be sterilized with boiling water: sulphite is not suitable as it corrodes the metal. During storage, screw-topped bottles must be stored upright with a one- or two-inch (three–four cm) air-space so that the wine is not in contact with the metal of the cap.

Wine bottles require corks, of course. Flanged or plastic-topped corks and plastic stoppers are suitable only as temporary stoppers, since they do not form a really tight seal. (The only exception is with sparkling wine bottles.) Much the best stoppers are cylindrical wine corks driven home using a simple hand-corking machine as illustrated in Fig. 6. The corks should be soaked in a bowl of weak sulphite solution overnight to soften them before use. Never boil corks or re-use second-hand ones, and make sure that they are of fine quality, with no cracks, cavities or blemishes in them. There is nothing more irritating than to have a carefully bottled wine seeping through the cork!

Fig 6: Two simple hand corking machines

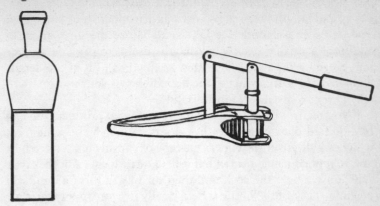

As anyone who has tried to get corks into wine bottles will know, a simple corking machine is essential, even for a few bottles of wine! The wooden hand-corker shown on the left is simple, cheap and very effective. The moistened corks are placed in a central tube and the body of the corker is located over the wine bottle. The plunger is hammered home, thus compressing the cork and driving it into the neck of the bottle. It is a machine I recommend highly. Rather more expensive and sophisticated, but perhaps a little easier to use, the metal corking gun on the right uses a mechanical piston to compress the cork and drive it home.

Unlike screw-topped bottles, corked wine bottles must be stored on their sides to keep the corks moist and swollen. A wine rack of some sort is obviously helpful in storage; suitable designs can be purchased quite cheaply or easily made at home from scrap wood.

PRESENTATION

The confusion that can arise if a bottle is not labelled clearly is almost unbelievable! And since labelling is necessary, why not add to the attractiveness of the finished bottle by sticking on a proper wine label? A wide selection is now available, printed in several colours with a variety of designs and printing to suit almost any type of wine.

A large label on the body of the bottle is best positioned *between* the seams, not across them. Ready gummed labels tend to dry and fall off with age, so use a little rubber solution glue on each edge and smooth the label out before the glue dries. In addition, a smaller neck label may be useful to provide a space for recording the date of production. You can fill in the details on blank labels according to the ingredients or your imagination, whichever seems most appropriate!

If you really wish to emulate the commercial product, you can fit coloured plastic capsules in colours to match the wine (red, white or gold) over the cork. One type of capsule has a stretch fit and is applied using a small hand-held "capsuler". Another type slips loosely over the cork and then shrinks to form a tight seal when the neck of the bottle is held briefly in a stream of warm air or a jet of steam.

SERVING WINE

You will be impatient to try your wine, once it has been bottled. But do keep at least some to mature; the improvement with time will probably surprise you. A useful scheme is to balance your rate of production and consumption, so that as each batch of mature wine from your storage area is consumed, another batch of new wine is ready to begin its maturation. In this way, you can select those wines which seem most promising and reserve them for longer maturing and use on special occasions; the other wines can be used for everyday drinking.

But whatever the occasion, try to suit your wine to the occasion and to those who are drinking it with you — not everyone likes dry wines, for example. Equally, conventions about the matching of food and wine are not merely foibles of the wine-snob, but have a sound basis. A sweet wine is quite acceptable with dessert, but hardly appropriate for meat or fish; equally, red wine spoils the taste of fish (or vice versa). Light meats such as poultry are best accompanied by medium-dry or dry white wines, although a light red can be equally acceptable.

The "heavier" meats and game need more robust and drier reds of the Burgundy and Bordeaux types. A dryish champagne is often served throughout a meal, and almost any wine seems suitable with cheese.

Once you have selected a wine, your enjoyment can be increased by following the guidelines for the journey from "cellar" to table. White and rosé wines are usually free of deposit and can be served from the bottle, but are all the better if they are chilled to about 10°C before being served. Red wines, on the other hand, often throw a deposit during storage. This sediment would be disturbed if the wine were to be served from the bottle, so it is best to decant the wine before use. This also enables the wine to "breathe": the exposure to air allows any odours formed during bottle storage to disperse and lifts the bouquet. All reds should be served at room temperature.

Incidentally, the best way of removing a cork is to use a double lever or wooden-handled double-screw corkscrew. These remove a cork by steady leverage which does not disturb any sediment.

Serve the wine in a glass which shows it off to best advantage: classic red wine glasses are almost spherical, and usually filled only half-full so that the bouquet can be enjoyed before the wine is tasted. In theory white wines should be served from long-stemmed glasses so that the heat of the hand does not remove the chill from the wine, but this is hardly a matter of overriding importance. Sparkling wines can be chilled and served from fluted glasses (rather than the traditional saucer-shaped ones) to preserve the bubbles and stop the wine quickly going flat.

THE APPRECIATION OF WINE

Too much has already been written by others on this subject. My view is simple — if a wine pleases *you*, then you have succeeded in what you set out to do. And this applies no matter how inexperienced or critical you may be. Greater discrimination of faults and preferences comes quickly, and your first few batches of wine should provide all the experience you need to make a drink which fulfils all your requirements — whatever they may be.

If you want to assess your own wine by the standards of commercial wine, buy a few bottles from a reputable supplier and spend some time comparing and contrasting the "real thing" with your vintages. If, on the other hand, you wish to assess your wine in its own right, here are the points to observe:

1. CLARITY AND COLOUR

Is the wine free of even the slightest haze or sediment?
If it has been sweetened, has all the sugar dissolved?
Is the colour pleasing to the eye?

2. BOUQUET

Inhale the bouquet and evaluate its quality:
Is it free from all off-putting smells?
Is it pronounced or barely noticeable?
Does the bouquet hint of the fruitiness of the wine?
Does it smell acidic or sweet?

3. FLAVOUR

And now the most important test of all:
Is the balance of the wine correct, i.e. does the level of acidity match the sweetness? Do the flavours of the ingredients blend together well?
Is the astringency too pronounced or completely lacking?
Is the wine free of all off-flavours?
What is the sensation after swallowing (the "farewell")?
Is the alcoholic strength correct?

In a word, therefore: enjoy your wine to the full, but always strive to improve your standards. In doing so, it may be helpful to refer occasionally to a table of . . .

PROBLEMS, FAULTS AND REMEDIES

Even with care, the use of correct procedures and attention to detail, faults sometimes still develop. So I have included the most common faults and remedies in this section.

FERMENTATION WILL NOT START

Always allow at least twelve hours between the addition of yeast and the first active signs of fermentation. If it is clear that the must will not ferment, there are several possible reasons:

1. *The must contains too much sugar and the yeast has been inhibited.* Remedy: Dilute with water until the S.G. is below 1.100 (approximately 2¾ lb sugar per gallon or 1.25 kg per 4.5 litres).

2. *Insufficient acid.* Taste the must, and if lacking in acid, add 2 teaspoonfuls of citric acid per gallon (4.5 litres) or adjust to pH 3.3.

3. *Too much acid.* Unlikely, but if the pH is less than 3.0, the yeast may have been killed or inhibited. Remedy: Dilute the must to reduce the acidity. Alternatively, neutralize the acid by adding potassium carbonate solution. Method: Dissolve 2 oz potassium carbonate in ¼ pint of water (60 g in 150 ml) and add to must a little at a time, stirring well and tasting after each addition until the acidity is correct. Note: 3 teaspoons of this solution will reduce the acidity of 1 gallon (4.5 litres) by about 1 ppt.

4. *Insufficient nutrient.* Remedy: Add the recommended dose of a good brand of nutrient together with two vitamin B_1 tablets per gallon (4.5 litres).

5. *Must is too cold.* Remedy: Move it into a temperature of 20°–25°C (68°–77°F).

6. *Must is too hot.* The yeast will be destroyed if it is added to a must at a temperature of over 30°C (86°F). Remedy: Prepare a new yeast starter and add it to the cool must.

7. *Yeast inactive.* If any sulphite is added to a must, the yeast must be introduced 24 hours later or it will be killed. Remedy: Make up a fresh starter and add it to the must.

FERMENTATION STARTS BUT SOON STOPS
("STUCK" FERMENTATION)

This usually happens because the yeast is weakened by excess sugar and can then tolerate only low levels of alcohol. Other causes include all those listed above. Remedy: Agitate the must by pouring it into a new container. Make up a fresh yeast starter and after it is established, add an equal quantity of must. Wait until fermentation is vigorous, then add same volume of must, and so on, until the whole is fermenting again.

WINE IS TOO SWEET

With low level of alcohol, indicates a "stuck ferment": see above. *With high level of alcohol*, suggests a complete fermentation up to the limit of the yeast's tolerance of alcohol. Remedy: Blend with a dry wine and use less sugar in the must next time.

WINE IS TOO ACID

Remedy: Reduce acidity of a finished wine by using a "Wine Acid Reduction Solution" *or* potassium carbonate solution as described in 3 above.

WINE HAS AN "OFF-FLAVOUR" OR UNPLEASANT
SMELL

The main causes of unpleasant flavours and odours in wine are listed below. Don't confuse these faults with the yeasty smell and taste of a wine which has not cleared completely.

1. *Mousey flavour*. Anyone who has experience of mice will know what this means! In fact the wine initially tastes sound, but leaves a nauseating after-taste on swallowing. Oddly, some people cannot detect this. Certainly caused by bacterial infection. Remedy: There is none. Throw the wine away and sterilize the equipment used.

2. *Medicinal flavour*. And it really does taste just like some medicines! Caused by a lack of acid in the must. Remedy: There is none. Throw the wine away and include more acid in the next must.

3. *Bad-egg smell.* May be caused by adding yeast to a sulphited must too soon (see page 26). Remedy: Try adding one Campden tablet per gallon (4.5 litres). If this has no effect, throw the wine away.

4. *Geranium smell.* Caused by using sorbate stabilizer without a Campden tablet. Follow the instructions on all such preparations. Remedy: There is none. Throw the wine away.

5. *Acetification or vinegar formation.* Self-explanatory. Caused by bacterial infection. Remedy: There is none. Pour the wine away. *Note:* Beginners sometimes confuse the bouquet of a bone-dry wine (especially apple) with the smell of acetic acid. Be sure that the wine is acetified by sweetening slightly and then tasting it.

6. *Other off-flavours.* These can be hard to identify. Caused by plastic or metallic equipment, detergents, an excessive amount of yeast nutrient, bacterial infection, leaving the wine in contact with dead yeast sediment or finings sediment, and so on. Such wine *may* be used for cooking, but is best thrown away.

WINE SMELLS OR TASTES LIKE SHERRY

Result of acetaldehyde formation due to presence of air (see page 81). Remedy: Try dissolving one or two Campden tablets in each gallon (4.5 litres). The problem can be avoided by ensuring that all storage containers are topped up.

WINE LACKS BOUQUET

Caused by a lack of acid in the must. The addition of 1 teaspoonful of lactic acid per gallon (4.5 litres) and further maturation *may* help.

WINE LACKS BODY

The body of a wine does not necessarily refer to its viscosity or thickness, but to the presence of enough fruit and an overall well balanced drink. A wine which is too "thin" and watery probably had too little fruit in the must. Remedy: Stir in a little concentrated grape juice. This will also sweeten the wine.

WINE TASTES FLAT OR INSIPID

Probably the result of too little tannin and/or acid. Remedy: Add a little extra tannin to taste.

WINE IS TOO ASTRINGENT OR BITTER

Astringency is the result of excess tannin. It is not the same as *bitterness*, which is much more likely to be a result of including sour or inappropriate ingredients such as citrus pith. Remedy: Excess tannin can be removed by fining with isinglass or longer maturation. Bitterness may be masked by adding up to 2 fl oz (60 ml) of glycerine per gallon (4.5 litres).

WINE WILL NOT CLEAR

There are several causes, the main ones being:

1. *Yeast in suspension.* Remedy: Move the wine to a cooler place and add the recommended dose of a stabilizer such as potassium sorbate (see page 93).

2. *Pectin haze.* Test for pectin haze by adding four parts of methylated spirit to one part of wine, mixing and leaving for thirty minutes. The formation of clots, strings or jelly indicates pectin in the wine. Remedy: Add a liquid pectic enzyme, ½ fl oz per gallon (40 ml per 4.5 litres) and leave until clear. Siphon off the sediment if necessary.

3. *Starch haze.* Test by adding a drop of brown iodine solution to a small volume of wine. A blue-black colouration indicates starch. Remedy: Add fungal amylase or diastase and leave until clear.

4. *Lactic acid bacteria infection.* This produces a thick, slimy or oily appearance. Remedy: Add two Campden tablets per gallon (4.5 litres), vigorously beat the wine with a spoon in a bucket and filter.

5. *Other hazes.* May be fined with bentonite. But if the wine has an odd colour or metallic flavour, throw it away.

REFERMENTATION

Sometimes a wine which has been transferred to bottle or storage vessel begins to ferment once again. This can occur if the wine was not allowed to ferment to dryness, not racked correctly, or bottled while still fermenting. It also happens if sucrose is added to sweeten a wine which still contains some live yeast cells. Clearly the production of carbon dioxide gas in bottle or storage vessel is inconvenient or even dangerous, with the risk of corks blowing out or burst bottles. There are several possible remedies. If the wine is still in bottles, and you wish to keep it there, you could replace the corks or stoppers with a safety-valve stopper. This is a neat plastic stopper that contains a ball valve in the form of a ball-bearing which lifts off its seat when pressure builds up and so allows any carbon dioxide gas produced in the bottle to escape. (Similar stoppers are available for demijohns, although · a rubber bung and air-lock would serve the same purpose.)

Another alternative would be to pour a small amount of wine out of each bottle and replace it with a wineglassful of brandy or vodka. This should increase the strength of the wine to the point where the yeast stops working. But better solutions to this problem would be to pour the wine back into a demijohn or storage vessel and either:

(a) Let the fermentation proceed to completion; or

(b) Add a stabilizer such as potassium sorbate. This is a very powerful inhibitor of mould and yeast growth; the recommended rate of use is 1 gram per gallon (4.5 litres), but it must be dissolved in the wine together with a Campden tablet, or a geranium smell may develop; or

(c) Filter the wine. This will remove all yeast cells and leave a clear, stable wine.

Above all, never try to stabilize a wine that has more than the slightest trace of fermentation by adding Campden tablets alone. The dose needed to kill a good wine yeast is about eight tablets per gallon — a level which would certainly spoil the wine, and might even be a health hazard. (Sodium metabisulphite is a poison, after all.) To reiterate the point, the main use of Campden tablets in a finished wine is to protect against bacterial infection and to prevent oxidation.

WINEMAKING WITH CONCENTRATED GRAPE JUICE AND "WINE KITS"

A common talking-point in winemaking circles concerns the relative merits of country wine and wine made from concentrated grape juice compound. In this section, therefore, I shall briefly describe the different varieties of concentrate which are available and consider the quality of the wine which they produce.

The first point to make is that the quality of the concentrated grape juices sold today is generally good, and consistent from year to year. The days of commercial vignerons deliberately using poor quality grapes unsuitable for their own wine in the preparation of concentrates have long since passed — chiefly due to the efforts of companies such as Southern Vinyards, Continental Wine Experts (CWE) and Boots.

The products sold by these companies and their competitors start life as ordinary, single strength grape juice in one of the world's winemaking regions — often Italy, Spain or Cyprus. Here it is stored until required, using sulphur dioxide as a preservative. It is then "flash" pasteurized, which removes much of the sulphur and sterilizes the juice, and subsequently concentrated under vacuum at 40°–50°C to a specific gravity of 1.325 or thereabouts. Vacuum concentration has the great advantage that it does not affect the flavour although careful control of heating at all stages is necessary to avoid caramelization of the sugar-rich juice.

When the concentrates reach this country, they should be blended to eliminate the variations in quality that inevitably occur from year to year. The bigger suppliers have produced ever more sophisticated and complex blends, combining grape concentrate with bulk additives such as glucose syrup and minor balancing agents such as tannin and lactic acid. These improvements have led to greater simplicity in winemaking and a more attractive end product.

Incidentally, the blended grape juice concentrates (which may now be called "compounds") are often sold together with other winemaking equipment such as yeast, Campden tablets and finings under the name "wine kits". There are also more sophisticated kits available which contain a full range of equipment, including wine bottles and demijohn. Obviously, the value of these kits depends partly on your experience and partly on how much you want to pay, but for a beginner they can be well worth the extra cost.

One of the biggest advantages of grape juice compounds is that they avoid the "cookery" aspect of country winemaking. They contain all the flavour, acid, nutrient and tannin required for winemaking. In theory, therefore, when the concentrate is diluted with water, fermented and cleared, it should produce a drink at least as good as some commercially produced wines (although that in itself may not be saying very much!) Nevertheless, it is obvious that the best quality grape juices are simply too expensive to use in concentrates, a fact which automatically sets a limit on the quality of the wine one can make. (On the other hand, of course, wine itself made from the very best grapes is also rather expensive and not an everyday drink.) The situation is different in the USA, where the excess of home-grown grapes allows the manufacture of high quality concentrates at a reasonable price.

Another important point for a beginner is that the failure rate (these do happen, unfortunately!) in winemaking with concentrates is lower than that in country winemaking. A good idea, therefore, is for a beginner to make two batches of wine on his first attempt: one from a concentrate, one from country ingredients. This raises the problem of which concentrate to use. There is certainly a bewildering variety available.

Perhaps the first decision should be whether you want a red, a white or a rosé, for this is a matter of personal taste. My own view is that the reds tend to be better, perhaps because the more delicate white grape juice does not lend itself quite so well to the concentration process.

Having made this decision, you must then select which quality you want to buy. There are really three types to choose from:

1) "Quick" wine concentrates: for producing wine in three or even two weeks.
2) "Standard" wine concentrates: the ones which require extra sugar to be added during fermentation (these may be labelled, confusingly, "fast fermenting").
3) "Superior" quality concentrates: these contain all the natural grape sugar needed for fermentation.

Of course, each of these varieties is available under the makers' own brand names.

QUICK WINE CONCENTRATES

The manufacturers claim that these products can produce wine in as little as three (sometimes even two!) weeks, but this raises an interesting paradox. In general, patience is the order of the day in winemaking. A slow, steady fermentation, time to clear, and time to mature are all important in adding to the finished quality. It follows, therefore, that a "quick" wine can never be as good as a standard one. The differences in preparation time between "quick" and "normal" grape juice compounds lie partly in the fermentation time, but mostly in the maturation time (or, rather, the lack of it). The fast fermenting compounds are formulated with added glucose sugar rather than the more complex sugars which would, in theory at any rate, require slightly longer to ferment. As far as maturation is concerned, the manufacturers add to the "quick" compounds various ingredients that are supposed to mimic the flavour of a matured wine so that it is drinkable at once. These ingredients vary from company to company, ranging from fruit juices and other flavourings to simple glucose compounds.

The whole subject is somewhat confusing, so I am grateful to CWE, who produce *Cellar 21*, a "three-week wine", for their comments: "In reality, almost all home-wine compounds producing table-wine strength (not more than 12% alcohol) are fairly fast fermenting. The main difference, in our opinion, is that three-week wines are *drinkable* so much sooner. In Cellar 21, our own range, fermentation starts promptly because of the method of reconstituting the yeast. The presence of relatively large amounts of nutrient in the compound, and the absence of the one or two varieties of grape concentrate which are characteristically slow fermenters, increases the speed of fermentation slightly. The unfermentable sugars in glucose syrup contribute a mellow roundness which makes the finished wine less harsh than, say, a freshly fermented Connoisseur's Choice type. (This is the Superior quality brand name used by CWE.)

But what of the taste and bouquet? You shouldn't expect much bouquet in a "quick" wine, but you may get a pleasantly quaffable plonk. Whether or not it can really be dignified by the word "wine" is a matter of opinion. It is worth mentioning that even these quick wines will improve to some extent with keeping — the manufacturer will probably mention a recommended time on the instruction leaflet.

STANDARD-QUALITY CONCENTRATES

This is the grape juice that needs the addition of some sugar during fermentation — usually 8 or 10 ounces per gallon (250–300 grams). It comes in a number of qualities ranging from simple, economical "House Red" and "House White" varieties to the better quality reds and whites identified by their descriptions: full-bodied red, medium red, dry red, dry full red, dry crisp white, sweet white, and so forth. These labels have generally replaced the older "regional" labels such as Bordeaux (Dry Red), Burgundy (Dry Full Red) and Chablis (Crisp Dry White), partly in response to pressure from winemaking regions of the EEC. The change seems sensible, for a grape compound can never produce the "real" wine of these varieties, only a similar type. In any event, a descriptive label is probably more useful for most winemakers, who may not be aware of the finer points of commercial wine labels.

But despite all this, the manufacturers do still try to blend their concentrates so they resemble commercially produced wine. This raises one possible criticism of standard kits: they sometimes produce a wine rather lacking in body. Certainly in comparative tastings these wines are confused with the real thing rather less often that the "superior" variety! However, they do provide a way of making enjoyable wine cheaply, without any fuss or mess; and they will definitely improve with keeping for a year or two. An important point: this is the concentrate to use if you add grape juice to your country wines.

If you have an urge to experiment, you might like to try the concentrates for making Vermouth and Sherry. In the first case, a sachet of powdered herbs is infused in the wine during fermentation to produce the characteristic vermouth flavour. This always seems to me to produce an unpleasantly strong flavour: my advice would be to put the herbs in a small, sterile nylon mesh bag and suspend this in the wine, tasting it every few days until you are happy with the result. The bag of herbs can then be removed. The sherry concentrates make a wine which has to be oxidized as described in Part 3 of this book. The problem here is that while you might get something resembling a cheap sherry bought in a shop, you might equally well get something completely undrinkable — the results are very variable, simply because of the complexity of making the wine.

Although vermouth and sherry may not be the ideal concentrates for a beginner, there is also a range of fruit concentrates which are cheap, great fun to make, and usually very successful. The range includes Blackberry, Elderberry, Grape and Bilberry, Grape and Cherry, Grape and Apricot, and many others. These come under the heading of standard concentrate because they need sugar adding; they are worth trying at least once.

SUPERIOR-QUALITY CONCENTRATES

These concentrates are the ones the connoisseur wants! Unfortunately, as one would expect, they are also more expensive (but still far cheaper than buying wine from the wine shop). These concentrates contain all the natural grape sugar needed to produce a normal table wine (although "dessert" varieties may need more sugar adding). All that is necessary is to open the can, pour the concentrate into a demijohn, add water and yeast, and leave it to ferment. In my opinion, the fermentation should be conducted at 20°–22°C (68°–72°F) even if this means it takes slightly longer: the subtle chemical changes responsible for bouquet and flavour take time to develop, and a slower fermentation helps. Moreover, a slow and steady fermentation resembles the commercial vigneron's work more than a quick one.

After fermentation and racking, the wine is left to clear, with the addition of a Campden tablet to protect against infection and oxidation. I do not really think it desirable to fine or filter these better quality compounds (although CWE recommend it for their Connoisseur's Choice, as do Southern Vinyards for their Grandalier). Given time, the wine should clear on its own, and it can then be racked again and bottled. Although you will doubtless succumb to the temptation to try some fairly soon, do keep as much as possible to mature. The reds certainly benefit from keeping — in my experience, for two years or more. The whites are ready much sooner, of course. When the time comes to drink the wine, serve the whites nicely chilled, and the reds at room temperature. Be careful not to disturb any sediment in the reds and open the bottles at least an hour before serving. Cheers!

PART 2

120 New Winemaking Recipes

The recipes in this section reflect the comprehensive range of winemaking ingredients now available. There are several general points which apply to all the recipes so, for the sake of convenience, I have listed them here.

- Many wines will foam vigorously when transferred to a demijohn, and so to avoid any overflow, any topping-up that is required should be done when the first violent fermentation has died away. (If at this stage you already have a full gallon of liquid, you can avoid the overflow by keeping a portion of the wine in a clean, sterile container beside the demijohn, adding it to the bulk when the fermentation has settled down.)

- Except in the case of dessert wines, the type of wine (i.e. social, table or aperitif) has generally not been specified. This is because the nature of the ingredients (and the information in the first part of the book) provide a guide to the type of wine to be made. In any case, the recipes are only a general guide and personal taste may dictate, for example, different amounts of sugar. Always remember that you can sweeten a dry wine to taste after fermentation, according to your personal taste.

- The length of pulp fermentation indicated in the recipe is measured from the time when signs of fermentation such as foaming or fruit rising to the surface first becomes visible.

- The quantities of ingredients measured in teaspoonfuls (tsp) always refer to level teaspoonfuls, unless the recipe indicates otherwise.

- When concentrated grape juice is called for in a country wine recipe, the variety to use is the "Standard" concentrate (as opposed to the quick fermenting ones and the ones which require no extra sugar).

A NOTE ABOUT MEASUREMENTS

The recipes show the quantities of ingredients in three systems of measurement: British (or Imperial), Metric and American. The conversion from British to Metric is fairly exact; where there is a discrepancy, it is insignificant and will not affect the results. By contrast, the quantities of ingredients specified in the American measurements are often smaller than the British or Metric ones. This is because the American gallon and pint are smaller than the British gallon and pint. (The unit of weight, the pound, is the same in both cases.) It follows that you should use one set of units — either British or Metric or American — throughout.

Should you need to convert from one system to another, the following information may be helpful:

British
20 fluid ounces (fl oz) = 1 pint
8 pints = 1 gallon
16 ounces (oz) = 1 pound (lb)

Metric
1000 millilitres (ml) = 1 litre

1000 gram (g) = 1 kilo (kg)

American
20 US fl oz = 1 US pint
8 US pints = 1 US gallon
16 oz = 1 lb

CONVERSION

British to Metric
1 pint = 568 ml
1 gallon = 4.5 litres
1 oz = 28 g
1 lb = 454 g

Metric to British
1 litre = 1¾ pints
100 ml = 3½ fl oz
1 kg = 2 lb 3 oz
100 g = 3½ oz

British to American
1 pint = 1.25 US pints
1 gallon = 10 US pints
(The pound is the same in both cases.)

APPLE WINE

In general, the sharper the flavour of the apples, the better the wine. Most winemakers use a mixture of "cooking" and "eating" apples, with perhaps a few crab apples as well. There are several ways of making apple wine; if, for example, you have a fruit crusher and press, you may wish to extract the juice from the fresh apples and ferment it directly. Alternatively, you could buy pure apple juice in cartons, and so avoid the fuss and mess of chopping and then pressing the apples. A second method is the standard pulp fermentation procedure. And yet another possibility is to boil the apples. All three methods are described below.

Whenever you are making apple wine, it is a good idea to add the recommended dose of a good brand of starch-destroying enzyme if the fruit is at all unripe. This will ensure that the finished wine clears properly. (See also Crab Apple Wine, page 124, Fruit Juice Wine, page 133, and White Wine, page 171.)

APPLE WINE (1)

	British	Metric	USA
Mixed apples	5 lb	2.3 kg	5 lb
Concentrated white grape juice	½ pt	300 ml	½ pt
Sugar	1¾ lb	800 g	1½ lb
Pectic enzyme			
Yeast and nutrient			
Water to	1 gallon	4.5 litres	1 gallon

Wash and cut up the whole apples, dropping the pieces into a pan containing about 6 pints (3.5 litres) of boiling water. Simmer the apple pieces gently for about 15–20 minutes. Then strain the liquid onto the sugar, and rinse the pulp with a little water. Add the grape concentrate, stir well to dissolve the sugar and leave to cool. When the temperature has fallen to about 20°C (68°F), add the pectic enzyme and a vigorously fermenting yeast starter. Transfer to a demijohn and plug loosely until the first violent fermentation has died down. Top up with cool boiled water to 1 gallon (4.5 litres), fit an air-lock and ferment out to dryness. Rack as normal and store for at least three months before bottling.

APPLE WINE (2)

For 2 gallons (9 litres) of
light, dry wine:

	British	Metric	USA
Apples	16 lb	7.5 kg	13 lb
Sugar	4¼ lb	2 kg	3½ lb
Water (approximately)	12 pints	7 litres	12 pints

medium-bodied and flavoured wine:

Apples	20 lb	9 kg	16½ lb
Sugar	5½ lb	2.5 kg	4½ lb
Water (approximately)	10 pints	5.5 litres	10 pints

full-bodied and flavoured wine:

Apples	24 lb	11 kg	20 lb
Sugar	5½ lb	2.5 kg	4½lb
Water (approximately)	8 pints	4.5 litres	8 pints

Plus: Pectic enzyme
Yeast and nutrient

These quantities may be halved for 1-gallon (4.5 litres) batches.

Wash the apples and chop, mash or crush them, dropping them immediately into a bin containing half the quantity of water indicated in the recipe (the exact amount of water required will only become clear when the apple pulp is pressed and the liquid strained off the solid). Dissolve a crushed Campden tablet in the water and leave for 24 hours. Then stir in 2 lb (900 g) of the sugar dissolved in 1 pint (550 ml) of boiling water. When cool, add the pectic enzyme and a yeast starter. Ferment on the pulp for 5 days, keeping well covered and stirring twice daily. Strain the liquid into a 2-gallon jar, or divide it between two 1-gallon jars. The fruit pulp should be pressed if possible to extract the maximum liquid. Divide the remainder of the sugar between the two jars and top up with water to about one inch below the neck of the jar. Ferment out to dryness under an air-lock, rack and store for three months before bottling. The wine should then be ready to drink but will improve if kept in bottle for three months before use.

Notes

- It is wise to taste the must to check the acidity, although if sharp-tasting apples have been used, no extra should be needed.

- If you don't have a wine press, you could add *Rohament P* (see page 36) to the must; this will break down the apple tissue which can then be strained from the pulp.

- As a rough guide, 12–14 lb (5.4–6.4 kg) of apples should yield about 4 pints (2.3 litres) of juice.

APPLE WINE (3)

	British	Metric	USA
Pure, unsweetened apple juice	2½–3½ pints	1.5–2 litres	2½–3½ pints
or Concentrated apple juice	1 pint	550 ml	1 pint
Sugar	2¼ lb	1 kg	1¾ lb
Citric acid	½ tsp	½ tsp	½ tsp
Yeast and nutrient			
Water to	1 gallon	4.5 litres	1 gallon

Prepare a yeast starter bottle the day before making the wine. When it is ready, dissolve the sugar in 2 pints (1.2 litres) of water, add to the apple juice or concentrate in a demijohn and top up to 7 pints (4 litres) with cool water. Check that the temperature is correct (20°C, 68°F) and introduce the yeast starter. Plug the jar loosely until the first violent fermentation has died down, then top up to the base of the neck, fit an air-lock and ferment out. Rack as normal; the wine may be topped up with water or pure apple juice and should be ready for drinking amost immediately.

Notes

- The strength and flavour of the wine depend on the amount of juice used; clearly this is a matter for personal taste, but as a guide, 3 pints (1.7 litres) of juice and 2¼ lb (1 kg) of sugar should make a medium table wine.

- If you obtain the juice yourself by pressing chopped fresh apples, strain it carefully to extract any fruit pulp and add pectic enzyme. Try not to expose the juice to the air or it may turn brown.

APPLE-BASED WINES

Apple blends well with many other fruits, and thus provides great opportunity for making up your own recipes. Some suggested recipes:

APPLE AND BILBERRY

	British	Metric	USA
Mixed apples (see notes below)	6 lb	2.7 kg	5 lb
Bilberries (fresh or bottled)	2 lb	900 g	2 lb
Sugar	2½ lb	1.15 kg	2 lb
Tartaric acid	½ tsp	½ tsp	½tsp
Pectic enzyme			
Yeast and nutrient			
Water to	1 gallon	4.5 litres	1 gallon

Wash the fruit carefully, mash or slice the apples and place all the fruit in a fermentation bin. Dissolve half the sugar in about 5 pints (2.8 litres) of boiling water, and pour the solution over the fruit. Crush the berries and leave to cool. When at 20°C (68°F), add the pectic enzyme and a yeast starter. Cover and ferment on pulp for 5 days, stirring twice daily. Strain the liquid from the pulp, pressing gently to extract as much juice as possible. Stir in the remainder of the sugar and transfer to a demijohn. Top up when first violent fermentation has died down, fit air-lock and ferment out. Rack and bottle as normal.

Notes

- Dried bilberries may be used; 8 oz (225 g) should be ample.
- Protect all red wines from the light or they will lose their colour.
- Suggested minimum storage times: Apple and Bilberry — six months; Apple and Blackberry (see below) — three months; Apple and Blackcurrant (see overleaf) — three months; Apple and Elderberry (see overleaf) six to nine months.
- 2 pints (1.2 litres) of pure apple juice could be used in place of fresh apples in all these recipes.

APPLE AND BLACKBERRY

	British	Metric	USA
Mixed apples	6 lb	2.7 kg	5 lb
Blackberries	3 lb	1.35 kg	3 lb
Sugar	2½ lb	1.15 kg	2 lb
Tartaric acid	½ tsp	½ tsp	½ tsp
Pectic enzyme			
Yeast and nutrient			
Water to	1 gallon	4.5 litres	1 gallon

Method as for Apple and Bilberry. (Canned blackberries may be used in this recipe, in which case reduce the sugar to 2¼ lb/1 kg.)

APPLE AND BLACKCURRANT

	British	Metric	USA
Pure apple juice	2 pints	1.2 litres	2 pints
Ribena blackcurrant concentrate	12 fl oz	360 ml	½ pint
Sugar	2¼ lb	1 kg	1¾ lb
Yeast and nutrient			
Water to	1 gallon	4.5 litres	1 gallon

Dissolve the sugar and Ribena in 3 pints (1.7 litres) of boiling water. Add the apple juice and transfer to a demijohn. Allow to cool, then introduce a vigorous yeast starter and top up to 1 gallon (4.5 litres). Fit an air-lock and ferment to dryness. A delicious light red wine suitable for drinking almost at once.

APPLE AND ELDERBERRY

	British	Metric	USA
Mixed apples	6 lb	2.7 kg	5 lb
Fresh elderberries	1½ lb	700 g	1½ lb
Sugar	2½ lb	1.15 kg	2 lb
Tartaric acid	½ tsp	½ tsp	½ tsp
Pectic enzyme			
Yeast and nutrient			
Water to	1 gallon	4.5 litres	1 gallon

Method as for Apple and Bilberry, page 105. (Dried elderberries may be used; 8 oz (225 g) should be ample.)

APRICOT WINE (1)

	British	Metric	USA
Stoned, fresh apricots	4 lb	1.8 kg	3½ lb
Sugar	2½ lb	1.15 kg	2 lb
Concentrated white grape juice	9 oz	250 g	⅓ pint

	British		
Citric acid	2 tsp	2 tsp	2 tsp
Grape tannin	¼ tsp	¼ tsp	¼ tsp
Pectic enzyme			
Yeast and nutrient			
Water to	1 gallon	4.5 litres	1 gallon

Put the fruit into a fermentation bin or bucket. Dissolve the sugar in 6 pints (3.5 litres) of boiling water and pour the solution over the fruit. Mash well, cover and leave to cool. Add the acid, tannin, grape concentrate and nutrient, together with a vigorously fermenting yeast starter. Ferment on pulp for 4 days, keeping well covered and stirring twice daily. Strain into a demijohn, top up with cool, boiled water if necessary, fit an air-lock and ferment to completion. Rack as necessary; the wine should be ready to drink after 6 months.

APRICOT WINE (2)

	British	Metric	USA
Dried apricots	1 lb	450 g	1 lb
or Tinned apricots	3 × 15½ oz cans	3 × 450g cans	2½ lb
or Apricot pulp, 1 can	2¼ lb	1 kg	1¾ lb
Sugar	2 lb	900 g	1¾ lb
Concentrated white grape juice	9 oz	250 g	⅓ pint
Citric acid	2 tsp	2 tsp	2 tsp
Grape tannin	¼ tsp	¼ tsp	¼ tsp
Pectic enzyme			
Yeast and nutrient			
Water to	1 gallon	4.5 litres	1 gallon

If using dried fruit, simmer the apricot pieces in 6 pints (3.5 litres) of water for 30 minutes. Dissolve the sugar in the hot liquid and transfer both fruit and liquid to a fermentation bin. *If using tinned fruit*, dissolve the sugar in 4 pints (2.3 litres) of boiling water and pour the solution over the fruit in a fermentation bin or bucket. Allow to cool, then add the acid, tannin, grape concentrate, nutrient and a vigorously fermenting yeast starter before making the volume up to 1 gallon (4.5 litres) with cool boiled water. Ferment on pulp for 2 days, then strain into demijohn, top up with water if necessary, fit air-lock and continue as normal.

BANANA WINE

	British	Metric	USA
Very ripe bananas	2½ lb	1.15 kg	2lb
Sultanas	12 oz	350 g	12 oz
Sugar	2 lb	900 g	1¾ lb
Citric acid	2 tsp	2 tsp	2 tsp
Grape tannin	½ tsp	½ tsp	½ tsp
Pectic enzyme			
Yeast and nutrient			
Water to	1 gallon	4.5 litres	1 gallon

Peel the bananas and discard the skins. (Whatever you may read about banana skins, they impart a most unpleasant taste to wine and should be avoided.) Chop the bananas into 4 pints (2.3 litres) of water and boil gently for 10 minutes. Then strain the liquid from the fruit. *Do not* squeeze the pulp. Boil the chopped sultanas in 2 pints (1.2 litres) of water for 10 minutes and strain off the liquid, squeezing the pulp gently to extract the maximum amount of liquid. Add it to the liquid from the bananas and stir in the sugar until completely dissolved. Allow to cool to 20°C (68°F), then add the acid, tannin, nutrient and pectic enzyme, together with a vigorously fermenting yeast starter. Transfer to a demijohn, top up to 1 gallon (4.5 litres) and fit an air-lock. Ferment to dryness and rack as normal.

Note:

- Do not exceed the recommended weight of bananas or the wine will need a long period of maturation and may have an unpleasantly strong flavour. This wine should be ready to drink soon after the final racking.

109

BANANA AND ELDERBERRY WINE

	British	Metric	USA
Fresh, peeled, ripe bananas	2 lb	900 g	1½ lb
or Dried bananas	10 oz	300 g	8 oz
Fresh elderberries	10 oz	300 g	8 oz
Sugar	2½ lb	1.15 kg	2 lb
Tartaric acid	2 tsp	2 tsp	2 tsp
Tannin	¼ tsp	¼ tsp	¼ tsp
Pectic enzyme			
Yeast and nutrient			
Water to	1 gallon	4.5 litres	1 gallon

Chop the bananas and boil them together with the elderberries for 5 minutes in 4 pints (2.3 litres) of water. Transfer fruit and liquid to a fermentation bin. Dissolve the sugar in 2 pints (1.2 litres) of hot water and add this to the fruit. When the must has cooled to fermentation temperature, add the acid, tannin, enzyme and yeast starter. Ferment on the pulp for 2 days, keeping well covered and stirring twice daily. Strain through fine mesh into a demijohn, top up with cool boiled water if necessary and fit an air-lock. The wine will probably ferment to dryness fairly quickly, although it will need storing for at least six months before use.

BANANA AND PARSNIP WINE

	British	Metric	USA
Bananas	2 lb	900 g	1½ lb
Parsnips	4 lb	1.8 kg	4 lb
Sugar	2 lb	1¼ kg	1¾ lb
Citric acid	3 tsp	3 tsp	3 tsp
Grape tannin	¼ tsp	¼ tsp	¼ tsp
Pectic enzyme			
Yeast and nutrient			

Water to		1 gallon	4.5 litres	1 gallon

Scrub the parsnips clean and cut off the tops but do not peel them. Cut them into smallish cubes and boil in 5 pints (2.8 litres) of water until the pieces are tender but not mushy. Strain the liquid (without pressing the chunks) onto the sugar and stir to dissolve. Allow to cool, then transfer to a demijohn. Boil the chopped, peeled bananas in 2 pints (1.2 litres) of water for 10 minutes and then strain the liquid into the demijohn, again without pressing the pulp, which can be discarded. Mix well, and when the must has cooled to fermentation temperature, add the acid, tannin, enzyme and a yeast starter. Plug with cotton wool until the foaming has died down, then fit an air-lock and ferment out in the normal way. The wine is drinkable at 6 months but vastly improved by keeping for a year.

BANANA AND TEA WINE
(Courtesy of Mr and Mrs A.G. McKay of
"The Village Home Brew", Edinburgh)

	British	Metric	USA
Dried bananas	9 oz	250 g	8 oz
Medium-strength tea	3 pints	1.7 litres	3 pints
Sugar	2¼ lb	1 kg	1¾ lb
Citric acid	1 heaped tsp	1 tsp	1 tsp
Tartaric acid	1 level tsp	1 tsp	1 tsp
Malic acid	1 level tsp	1 tsp	1 tsp
Pectolase			
Yeast and nutrient			

Chop up dried bananas into small pieces and place in a pan with 2½ pints (1.5 litres) of water. Bring to the boil and simmer for an hour until the bananas are mushy. Strain off into a gallon jar. There should be about 2 pints (1.2 litres) of liquid. Then add the 3 pints (1.7 litres) of tea and make up to 7 pints (4 litres) with the sugar dissolved in 2 pints (1.2 litres) of water. When the liquid in the jar is around 67°F–75°F (20°–25°C) add the yeast and other ingredients. Fit an air-lock and when the first violent fermentation has died down top up to the gallon with cooled boiled water. Allow to ferment out and rack off as normal. Sweeten to taste.

BARLEY WINE

This is not the strong beer of the same name, but wine made with barley cereal!

	British	Metric	USA
Barley (grain)	2 lb	900 g	2 lb
Concentrated white grape juice	⅔ pint	400 ml	⅔ pint
Sugar	1¾ lb	800 g	1½ lb
or			
Sultanas	1 lb	450 g	12 oz
Sugar	2 lb	900 g	1¾ lb
Grape tannin	¼ tsp	¼ tsp	¼ tsp

Juice of 2 lemons

Fungal amylase or diastase

Pectic enzyme (with sultanas)

Yeast and nutrient

Water to	1 gallon	4.5 litres	1 gallon

Wash the barley and place it in a bucket with the chopped sultanas or grape concentrate. Pour 5 pints (2.8 litres) of boiling water over these ingredients, cover and leave to cool. At the normal fermentation temperature, add the lemon juice, tannin, fungal amylase and yeast starter. Ferment on the pulp for 5 days, then strain into a demijohn and add the sugar dissolved in enough water to bring the volume up to 1 gallon (4.5 litres). Fit air-lock and ferment out in the normal way. Cereal wines take longer than average to mature, although the inclusion of only 2 lb (900 g) of grain should help to reduce this. Store for six to nine months in bottle after final racking.

BEETROOT WINE

	British	Metric	USA
Young, fresh beetroot	4 lb	1.8 kg	3½ lb
Concentrated red grape juice	½ pint	300 ml	½ pint
Sugar	2 lb	900 g	1¾ lb
Root ginger		2 or 3 pieces	
Tannin	½ tsp	½ tsp	½ tsp
Citric or tartaric acid	2 tsp	2 tsp	2 tsp
Fungal amylase or diastase			
Yeast and nutrient			
Water to	1 gallon	4.5 litres	1 gallon

Scrub the beetroot but do not peel them. They should be young and fresh, otherwise the wine may taste earthy. Chop them into chunks and simmer together with the ginger in 6 pints (3.5 litres) of unsalted water until the pieces are tender but not mushy; this may take up to an hour or even more. Strain off the liquid — the solids are not required — and add the sugar and concentrate, stirring well to ensure they dissolve. Allow to cool, then add the other ingredients, top up as necessary and place in a demijohn under air-lock. Ferment out in normal way. Beetroot is very suited to producing a strong sweet wine, so if desired extra sugar can be dissolved in the wine 4 oz (110 g) at a time until the required sweetness and strength are obtained. This is a good tasting wine but requires up to two years' storage before it is at its best.

Note

- All red wines lose their colour in sunlight, but this applies especially to beetroot. Use fermentation vessels made of dark glass or wrap thick brown paper around colourless ones.

BEETROOT AND PINEAPPLE WINE

This sounds like an unusual combination, but the result is said to be very good.

	British	Metric	USA
Fresh, young beetroot	3 lb	1.35 kg	2½ lb
Canned pineapple	2 × 15½ oz cans	2 × 450 g cans	2 lb
Sugar	2¼ lb	1 kg	1¾ lb
Citric acid	1 tsp	1 tsp	1 tsp
Grape tannin	¼ tsp	¼ tsp	¼ tsp
Pectic enzyme			
Yeast and nutrient			
Water to	1 gallon	4.5 litres	1 gallon

Scrub and slice the beetroot and simmer until tender. Strain the liquid onto the pineapple in a fermentation bin — the beetroot chunks are not required — and mash the pineapple. Dissolve the sugar in 2 pints (1.2 litres) of water, add to the fruit and make up the volume to one gallon (4.5 litres). Allow to cool before adding the acid, tannin and enzyme together with a yeast starter. Ferment on the pulp for one week before straining into a demijohn. Top up with water if necessary, fit an air-lock and ferment out in the normal way. Store for 6 months before use.

BILBERRY (OR BLUEBERRY) TABLE WINE

	British	Metric	USA
Fresh bilberries	3 lb	1.35 kg	2½ lb
or Bottled or canned bilberries*	2 lb	900 g	2 lb
or Dried bilberries	12 oz	350 g	12 oz
Sugar	2½ lb	1.15 kg	2 lb
Tartaric acid	2 tsp	2 tsp	2 tsp
Pectic enzyme			
Yeast and nutrient			
Water to	1 gallon	4.5 litres	1 gallon

*Include 9 oz (225 g) of red or white grape concentrate with bottled or canned berries, and reduce the sugar to 2¼ lb (1 kg/USA 1¾ lb).

Wash both fresh and dried berries in water before use, being careful to remove all leaves, stalks and so on. If the fresh berries are small and sour, and with dried berries in any case, heat the berries in about 6 pints (3.5 litres) of water at 70°–80°C (160°–175°F) for 10–15 minutes. Otherwise pour 6 pints (3.5 litres) of boiling water over the fruit in a fermentation bin. Dissolve half the sugar in 1 pint (600 ml) of water and add to the fruit. When cool, add the acid, enzyme, yeast and nutrient. Ferment on the pulp for 4 days, keeping well covered and stirring twice daily. Strain through a fine mesh on to the remainder of the sugar and stir well to dissolve. Transfer to a demijohn, top up if necessary, fit an air-lock and ferment out as normal. Rack and bottle after six months' storage, and try to keep for at least another three months before use.

Note

- Bilberries produce the best British red wine — even better than elderberry. The range of recipes is enormous, and provides a great opportunity for experiment. The finished product is always very drinkable — and often delicious! Obviously the final strength and sweetness depend very much on your preference, but a good starting point is 3 lb (1.35 kg) of fresh bilberries and 2½ lb (1.15 kg) of sugar for a dry red table wine. (USA: 2½ lb berries and 2 lb sugar.) The amount of acid required does tend to be variable, depending chiefly on the amount of sunshine in a season.

BILBERRY DESSERT WINE

	British	Metric	USA
Fresh bilberries	3 lb	1.35 kg	2½ lb
Concentrated red grape juice	½ pint	300 ml	½ pint
Sugar	2¾ lb	1.25 kg	2¼ lb
Tartaric acid	2 tsp	2 tsp	2 tsp

Pectic enzyme

Yeast and nutrient

Water to   1 gallon   4.5 litres   1 gallon

Dissolve half the sugar in 5 pints (2.8 litres) of boiling water and pour the solution over the fruit. Mash the fruit well, cover and leave to cool. Stir in the grape concentrate, acid and enzyme, together with a yeast starter. Ferment on the pulp for 4 days, keeping well covered and stirring twice daily. Then strain through a fine mesh into a demijohn, top up to just under the gallon (4.5 litres) and fit an air-lock. Add the remaining sugar in small (4 oz/110 g) lots each time the fermentation dies down until the desired level of strength and sweetness has been achieved. Ensure that the wine is thoroughly mixed after each addition. Store for up to two years before use.

Note

- The addition of a little glycerol to this wine improves the body and aids maturation.

BLACKBERRY TABLE WINE

	British	*Metric*	*USA*
Fresh, ripe blackberries	4–5 lb	1.8–2.3 kg	3½–4 lb
Concentrated red grape juice	9 oz	250 g	⅓ pint
Sugar	2¼ lb	1 kg	1¾ lb
Citric acid	2 tsp	2 tsp	2 tsp
Grape tannin	¼ tsp	¼ tsp	¼ tsp
Pectin enzyme			
Yeast and nutrient			
Water to		1 gallon 4.5 litres 1 gallon	

Wash the berries and place them in a fermentation bin. Crush the berries and pour about 5 pints (2.8 litres) of boiling water over them. Cover and allow to cool. When the temperature has fallen to 20°C (68°F), add 1 pint (550 ml) of water in which 1 lb (450 g) of the sugar has been dissolved. Stir well, and add the tannin, acid, enzyme and a vigorous yeast starter. Cover and ferment on pulp for 4 days, stirring twice daily. Strain off the liquid into a demijohn, pressing the pulp very lightly to extract the maximum amount of juice. Add the remainder of the sugar dissolved in enough water to make the volume up to 1 gallon (4.5 litres) and mix well. The fermentation will be fairly rapid at a constant temperature; rack when it has finished and store for 6 months before bottling.

Notes

- Campden tablets can discolour this wine, so do not add more than one per gallon (4.5 litres) after racking. Before fermentation, the use of boiling water will both sterilize the fruit and extract its flavour.

- Do not expose the wine to sunlight or it will lose its glorious colour. Use dark glass jars and bottles or wrap brown paper around colourless ones.

- Although pulp fermentation is the traditional method of preparation, good results can also be achieved by heating the berries in water and then pressing to extract the juice (see page 29). This avoids the extraction of as much tannin and so produces a more mellow wine.

BLACKBERRY DESSERT WINE

	British	Metric	USA
Fresh ripe blackberries	4–5 lb	1.8–2.3 kg	4 lb
Concentrated red grape juice	¾ pint	425 ml	¾ pint
Sugar	2½ lb	1.15 kg	2 lb
Citric acid	1 tsp	1 tsp	1 tsp
Grape tannin	¼ tsp	¼ tsp	¼ tsp
Pectic enzyme			
Yeast and nutrient			
Water to	1 gallon	4.5 litres	1 gallon

Follow the method for Blackberry Table Wine, but add the second half of the sugar in 4-oz (110 g) lots until the desired degree of strength and sweetness is obtained. Store for at least eighteen months and preferably two years before use.

Note

- A little glycerol improves the body of this wine and aids maturation.

BLACKCURRANT WINE (1)

	British	*Metric*	*USA*
Fresh, ripe blackcurrants	3 lb	1.35 kg	2½ lb
Concentrated red grape juice	9 oz	250 g	⅓ pint
Sugar	2¼ lb	1 kg	1¾ lb
Pectic enzyme			
Yeast and nutrient			
Water to	1 gallon	4.5 litres	1 gallon

Follow the method as for Blackberry Table Wine, but do not add any acid or tannin.

BLACKCURRANT WINE (2)

	British	*Metric*	*USA*
Ribena blackcurrant concentrate	¾ pint	425 ml	¾ pint
Sugar	1½ lb	700 g	1½ lb
Concentrated red grape juice	9 oz	250 g	⅓ pint
or Liquid malt extract	8 oz	225 g	6 oz
Tartaric acid	¾ tsp	¾ tsp	¾ tsp
Grape tannin	⅛ tsp	⅛ tsp	⅛ tsp
Yeast and nutrient			
Water to	1 gallon	4.5 litres	1 gallon

Heat the Ribena and malt extract (if using it) in 4 pints (2.3 litres) of water to boiling point and simmer for 3 minutes to drive off any preservative. Dissolve the sugar in the liquid while it is still hot, add the concentrate (if using it) and allow to cool. At fermentation temperature, add the acid, tannin and a yeast starter before making the volume up to about 7½ pints (4.25 litres) in a demijohn. Fit an air-lock, and when the first violent fermentation has died down, top up to 1 gallon (4.5 litres) with cool boiled water. Fermentation should be rapid; when it has finished, the wine can be filtered to speed up the clearing process. It may be used at once or kept for six months, although little change will take place in the wine beyond that.

BLACKCURRANT AND CHERRY WINE

	British	Metric	USA
Blackcurrants	2 lb	900 g	2 lb
Red or black cherries	3 lb	1.35 kg	2½ lb
Concentrated grape juice	9 oz	250 g	⅓ pint
Sugar	2¼ lb	1 kg	1¾ lb
Pectic enzyme			
Yeast and nutrient			
Water to	1 gallon	4.5 litres	1 gallon

Wash the fruit and place it in a fermentation bin. Pour on 5 pints (2.8 litres) of boiling water and crush the fruit well. When cool, add 1 pint (550 ml) of water in which 1 lb (450 g) of the sugar has been dissolved. Add the pectic enzyme and a yeast starter. Ferment on the pulp for 5 days, keeping well covered and stirring twice daily. Strain into a demijohn, adding the remainder of the sugar dissolved in enough water to make the volume up to one gallon (4.5 litres). Fit an air lock and ferment to dryness; the wine will be ready almost at once.

CARROT WINE

	British	Metric	USA
Fresh carrots	4 lb	1.8 kg	3½ lb
Concentrated white grape juice	9 oz	250 g	⅓ pint

	British	Metric	USA
Sugar	2¼ lb	1 kg	1¾ lb
Juice of 3 lemons			
Grape tannin	½ tsp	½ tsp	½ tsp
Fungal amylase or diastase			
Yeast and nutrient			
Water to	1 gallon	4.5 litres	1 gallon

Scrub but do not peel the carrots and slice them into boiling water. Simmer until tender but not mushy — up to one hour. Strain the liquid onto the sugar and stir well to dissolve. Allow to cool, then add the concentrate, tannin, lemon juice and fungal amylase before making up to about 7½ pints (4.25 litres). Transfer to a demijohn and add a yeast starter. Fit an air-lock or plug loosely until the first violent fermentation has died down, then top up to base of neck with cool boiled water. Refit the air-lock and ferment out. The wine may be sweetened slightly; it is best as a medium dry wine. As with all vegetable wines, storage for at least twelve months from the end of fermentation is advisable.

CARROT AND WHEAT WINE

	British	Metric	USA
Carrots	2 lb	900 g	2 lb
Wheat (grain)	1 lb	450 g	12 oz
Sultanas	12 oz	350 g	8 oz
Sugar	2½ lb	1.15 kg	2 lb
Citric acid	3 tsp	3 tsp	3 tsp
Tannin	½ tsp	½ tsp	½ tsp
Pectic enzyme			
Fungal amylase or diastase			
Yeast and nutrient			
Water to	1 gallon	4.5 litres	1 gallon

Wash the wheat and place it in a bucket or bin. Pour 2 pints (1.2 litres) of hot water over it. Boil the carrots in 3 pints (1.7 litres) of water until they are tender but not mushy and strain the liquid onto the wheat. (The carrot pieces are not required.) Boil the sultanas for 10 minutes and add both fruit and liquid to the bin. Add the sugar and stir well to dissolve. When cool, add the enzymes, acid, tannin and a yeast starter before making the total volume up to 1 gallon (4.5 litres) with cool boiled water. Ferment on pulp for 3 days, keeping well covered and stirring twice daily. Strain into a demijohn, top up if necessary with cooled, boiled water and fit an air-lock. Ferment as normal, but sweeten the wine slightly after the final racking. Store for 6 months before use.

CHERRY WINE

	British	Metric	USA
Mixed cherries*	5–6 lb	2.3–2.7 kg	4–5 lb
Concentrated red grape juice	½ pint	300 ml	½ pint
Sugar	2 lb	900 g	1¾ lb
Tartaric acid	1 tsp	1 tsp	1 tsp
Grape tannin	¼ tsp	¼ tsp	¼ tsp
Pectic enzyme			
Yeast and nutrient			
Water to	1 gallon	4.5 litres	1 gallon

*This will produce a light red wine; the flavour and body may be improved by using a proportion of Morello cherries and increasing the weight of fruit up to as much as 8 lb (3.6 kg) per gallon (4.5 litres).

Remove all stalks and leaves etc., from the fruit and rinse well. Crush the fruit in a fermentation bin or bucket and pour on 6 pints (3.5 litres) of boiling water. (Be careful not to crack the stones.) Cover and allow to cool, then add the enzyme, acid, tannin, grape concentrate and half of the sugar. Stir well to dissolve. Introduce a vigorous yeast starter, and ferment on the pulp for 5 days, keeping well covered and stirring twice daily. After 5 days, strain onto the rest of the sugar and stir until it dissolves. Transfer to demijohn, fit an air-lock and ferment out. Sweeten to taste.

CLOVER WINE

	British	Metric	USA
Fresh red clover flowers (lightly pressed)	4 pints	2.3 litres	4 pints
or Packet dried clover flowers	2 oz	60 g	2 oz
Concentrated white grape juice	½ pint	300 ml	½ pint
Sugar	1¾ lb	800 g	1½ lb
Citric acid	1 tsp	1 tsp	1 tsp
Tannin	¼ tsp	¼ tsp	¼ tsp
Yeast and nutrient			
Water to	1 gallon	4.5 litres	1 gallon

Wash and rinse the flowers, being careful to remove any foreign matter such as leaves or twigs. Shake the petals dry in a colander and then transfer the flowers to a basin or bowl. Pour on 6 pints (3.5 litres) of hot (70°C/160°F) water and leave to cool. Dissolve one Campden tablet in the liquid and leave to infuse for 2 days. Then strain off the liquid, pressing the flowers gently to extract the maximum flavour. Add the grape concentrate, acid and tannin, together with a vigorous yeast starter. Transfer to a demijohn and fit an air-lock. When the first vigorous fermentation has died down, dissolve the remaining sugar in the wine and top up to 1 gallon (4.5 litres). Ferment out in the normal way, allow to clear and stabilize. Rack and sweeten to taste. All flower wines are probably best medium-dry or medium-sweet with fairly low alcohol content. There is no advantage to be gained from storing the wines for a long period and they can be consumed soon after the final racking

Notes

- Extra flavour will be extracted if the flowers are left in the must for the first day or so of fermentation.
- An alternative method is to wash and rinse the flowers, enclose them in a linen mesh bag and hang the bag in the fermenting must so that the essence can infuse into the wine.

COLTSFOOT WINE

	British	Metric	USA
Yellow coltsfoot flowers	4 pints	2.3 litres	4 pints
or Dried flowers, 1 packet	2 oz	60 g	2 oz
Concentrated white grape juice	½ pint	300 ml	½ pint
Sugar	1¾ lb	800 g	1½ lb
Citric acid	1 tsp	1 tsp	1 tsp
Grape tannin	¼ tsp	¼ tsp	¼ tsp
Yeast and nutrient			
Water to	1 gallon	4.5 litres	1 gallon

Method as for Clover Wine. Note, however, that you should include the minimum of green material or the wine will have an unpleasant flavour. This can be achieved by cutting the yellow petals off the green flower-base with a pair of scissors.

COWSLIP WINE

This was one of the best of all country wines; sadly, however, the flowers are now extremely rare, and so protected by legislation. However, if you can find the dried variety, you could try making the wine. See the methods described for Elderflower Wine. 2 oz (60 g) of dried flowers would be enough for 1 gallon (4.5 litres) of wine.

CRAB APPLE WINE

Only the red or red-and-cream coloured apples are suitable for winemaking.

For each gallon (4.5 litres) of wine:

	British	Metric	USA
Ripe crab apples	8 lb	3.6 kg	6½ lb
Sugar	2½ lb	1.15 kg	2 lb
Pectic enzyme			
Rohament P			
Yeast and nutrient			
Water	as required		

Wash the apples, and chop, crush or mince them. This can be done with an electric juice extractor, liquidizer, chip-making machine, a stout wooden mallet (with the apples in polythene bags), or something similar. As the apples are crushed, place the fruit pulp or pieces in a bucket containing 4 pints (2.3 litres) of water in which one Campden tablet has been dissolved. Dissolve some pectic enzyme and Rohament P in the apple/water mixture. This will break down the fruit tissue and aid the extraction of flavour. Twenty-four hours later, dissolve half the sugar in the water and add a yeast starter. Ferment on the pulp for 5 days, keeping well covered and stirring twice daily. Then strain and press the pulp gently to extract the maximum amount of juice; dissolve the remainder of the sugar in the juice, transfer to a demijohn and top up if necessary with cool boiled water. Fit an air-lock and ferment to dryness. Rack when the wine is clear and a firm deposit has formed.

Notes
- An alternative method of juice extraction is to deep freeze the apples before use. This will rupture the structure of the tissue and allow the juice to run freely when the apples are thawed and mashed.

- Crab apples can be very acidic. It is therefore a good idea to check the acidity and adjust it if necessary. (See page 89.)

CRAB APPLE AND BERRY WINE

"HEDGEROW WINE"

(By Edith Middleton, Leicester Circle Winner)

	British	Metric	USA
Crab apples	4 lb	1.8 kg	4 lb
Hawthorn berries	8 oz	225 g	4 oz
Blackberries and elderberries	2 lb	900 g	1¾ lb
Sugar	2½ lb	1.15 kg	2 lb
Juice of 1 lemon			
Pectolase			
Yeast and nutrient			
Water to	1 gallon	4.5 litres	1 gallon

Wash the crab apples, chop them up, and boil for 10 minutes. Strip hawthorn berries, blackberries and elderberries from stalks. Mash together. Pour crab apples over rest of fruit. Add the sugar and lemon juice, make up to 1 gallon (4.5 litres) with cold water. When cool add yeast and pectic enzyme. Ferment in bucket for three days, keeping well covered and stirring vigorously twice a day. Strain through muslin or clean cloth into gallon jar, ferment till clear. Rack and bottle as normal.

CRAB APPLE AND SLOE WINE

(By Mr H. Gibbs of Lincoln)

		British	Metric	USA
Crab apples	both frozen	4 lb	1.8 kg	4 lb
Sloes	before use	2 lb	900 g	1½ lb

125

Wheat	6 oz	170 g	6 oz
Raisins	9 oz	250 g	6 oz
Sugar	3 lb	1.35 kg	2½ lb
Malt extract	4 oz	110 g	4 oz
Pectic enzyme			
Yeast and nutrient			
Water to	1 gallon	4.5 litres	1 gallon

Defrost fruit and place in a bucket. Crush with hands. Add wheat, minced raisins, sugar dissolved in water, pectic enzyme, one Campden tablet and malt extract. Stir well, cover and leave for 24 hours, then add yeast and nutrient. Leave on pulp for 7 days, keeping well covered and stirring twice daily. Strain into demijohn and fit air-lock. Ferment out in usual way. Rack at least twice and store for 6 months in a demijohn after the wine has cleared before drinking it.

DAMSON TABLE WINE (1)

	British	Metric	USA
Fresh ripe damsons	4 lb	1.8 kg	4 lb
Sugar	2½ lb	1.15 kg	2 lb
Tartaric acid	1 tsp	1 tsp	1 tsp
Pectic enzyme			
Yeast and nutrient			
Water to	1 gallon	4.5 litres	1 gallon

Wash the fruit and place it in a fermentation bin. Crush well, then pour on 5 pints (2.8 litres) of boiling water and cover. Allow to cool, then add the sugar dissolved in enough water to bring the volume up to 1 gallon (4.5 litres), together with the acid, enzyme and yeast. Ferment on pulp for 4 days, keeping well covered and stirring twice daily. Strain into a demijohn, top up with cool boiled water to base of neck, fit air-lock and ferment to dryness. Rack when fermentation has ended and the wine has cleared in normal way.

Note

- Protect this wine from sunlight or it will lose its colour. The use of sulphite can also discolour the wine, and should be kept to a minimum.

DAMSON TABLE WINE (2)

	British	Metric	USA
Fresh ripe damsons	3 lb	1.35 kg	3 lb
Concentrated red grape juice	½ pint	300 ml	½ pint
Sugar	2 lb	900 g	1¾ lb
Tartaric acid	1 tsp	1 tsp	1 tsp
Pectic enzyme			
Yeast and nutrient			
Water to	1 gallon	4.5 litres	1 gallon

Wash the damsons and then drop them into about 5 pints (2.8 litres) of water at 70°–80°C (160°–175°F). Maintain this temperature for 10–15 minutes, crushing the fruit with a wooden spoon and stirring continuously. Then pour the fruit and liquid into a straining bag, positioned so that the liquid runs onto the sugar. Do not press the pulp hard, or the fruit will become puréed. (If necessary, the pulp can be washed through with a little cold water.) Once the pulp is dry, it can be discarded. Stir the liquid to dissolve the sugar and add the concentrate before making up to 1 gallon (4.5 litres) with cool, boiled water. When the temperature has fallen to 20°C (68°F) add the yeast and transfer to a demijohn. Plug with cotton wool until the first violent fermentation has died away, then top up if necessary, fit an air-lock and ferment out in the normal way.

127

DAMSON DESSERT WINE

	British	Metric	USA
Fresh ripe damsons	4½ lb	2 kg	4 lb
Concentrated red grape juice	⅔ pt	400 ml	⅔ pint
Bananas	1 lb	450 g	8 oz
Sugar	2¼ lb	1 kg	1¾ lb
Tartaric acid	1½ tsp	1½ tsp	1½ tsp
Pectic enzyme			
Yeast and nutrient			
Water to	1 gallon	4.5 litres	1 gallon

Boil the peeled, sliced bananas in 5 pints (2.8 litres) of water until they are soft. Strain the liquid onto 1 lb (450 g) of the sugar and stir well until dissolved. Reheat the liquid to boiling point and then pour it over the crushed, washed damsons in a fermentation bin. Cover and allow to cool. Add the concentrate, acid, pectic enzyme and make the volume up to about 7 pints (4 litres) before introducing a yeast starter. Mix well, cover and ferment on pulp for 5 days, stirring twice daily. Strain into a demijohn, pressing the pulp lightly. Fit an air-lock and carry on fermentation in the normal way, adding the remaining sugar in 4-oz
(110 g) lots each time fermentation slows until the desired strength and sweetness have been achieved. Rack and store for 9 months in demijohn if possible before bottling and another 9 months in bottle before use. This is a wine which improves very much with age and you should try to keep it as long as possible.

DAMSON AND SLOE WINE

(Courtesy of Leicester Amateur Wine Circle)

	British	Metric	USA
Damsons	2 lb	900 g	2 lb
Sloes	1 lb	450 g	12 oz

Minced raisins	1 lb	450 g	12 oz
Sugar	1½ lb	700 g	1½ lb
Pectolase			
Yeast and nutrient			
Water to	1 gallon	4.5 litres	1 gallon

Put fruit in a plastic bucket, pour over 6 pints (3.5 litres) of cold water and crush fruit. Add the minced raisins, nutrient, pectolase and 2 Campden tablets. Cover and leave for 2 days. Add the sugar and yeast, ferment on pulp for 3 days, keeping well covered and stirring daily. Strain into jar, fit lock and ferment out as normal. Rack when clear.

DANDELION WINE

	British	Metric	USA
Dandelion flowers, lightly pressed	4 pints	2.3 litres	4 pints
or 1 packet dried flowers	2 oz	60 g	2 oz
Concentrated white grape juice	½ pint	300 ml	½ pint
Sugar	1¾ lb	800 g	1½ lb
Citric acid	1 tsp	1 tsp	1 tsp
Grape tannin	¼ tsp	¼ tsp	¼ tsp
Yeast and nutrient			
Water to	1 gallon	4.5 litres	1 gallon

Do not include much greenery or the flavour will be impaired. Method as for Coltsfoot Wine, page 123.

DATE WINE

	British	Metric	USA
Dried, stoned dates	2 lb	900 g	1¾ lb
Sugar	1¾ lb	800 g	1½ lb
Juice of 3 lemons and 2 oranges			
Grape tannin	½ tsp	½ tsp	½ tsp

Pectic enzyme

Yeast and nutrient

Water to		1 gallon	4.5 litres 1 gallon

Wash the fruit and chop it up. Place the pieces in a fermentation bin and add 6 pints (3.5 litres) of boiling water. Dissolve the sugar in 1 pint (500 ml) of water and add this to the bin, together with the juice and tannin. Allow to cool, then add the pectic enzyme and yeast. Stir well and cover. Ferment on the pulp for 5 days and then strain through a coarse and subsequently a fine mesh straining bag into a demijohn. Top up if necessary with water; also check the acidity and, if it seems deficient, add a little citric acid. Fit an air-lock and ferment out in the normal way. Rack when the wine begins to clear and again when it has cleared completely. Store for six months before use. An unusual but pleasant wine.

(1) "ELDERBERRY BURGUNDY"
(By Mr Gordon Durham of Garstang Wine Circle)

	British	Metric	USA
Dried elderberries	8 oz	225 g	6 oz
Dried bananas	6 oz	170 g	6 oz
Sultanas	8 oz	225 g	6 oz
Sugar	1½ lb	700 g	1½ lb
Citric acid	1 tsp	1 tsp	1 tsp
Tartaric acid	1 tsp	1 tsp	1 tsp
Pectolase			
Yeast and nutrient			
Water to	1 gallon	4.5 litres	1 gallon

Make up a starter bottle. Wash all dried ingredients and place in bucket with sugar. Add 7 pints (4 litres) of boiling water and stir well. Cover well and leave to cool, then add a crushed Campden tablet. Twenty-four hours later add pectolase, yeast starter and nutrient. Ferment on pulp for 6 days, stirring daily. Strain into demijohn, fir air-lock and ferment to dryness.

(2) ELDERBERRY TABLE WINE

	British	Metric	USA
Fresh elderberries	3 lb	1.35 kg	2½ lb
Sugar	2¼ lb	1 kg	1¾ lb
Tartaric acid	2 tsp	2 tsp	2 tsp
Pectic enzyme			
Yeast and nutrient			
Water to	1 gallon	4.5 litres	1 gallon

Wash the elderberries and strip them from their stalks by running a fork down the stalks through the bunches of berries. Place the berries in 5 pints (2.8 litres) of water and heat to boiling point. Simmer gently for 5 minutes, then pour the fruit and liquid into a straining bag and express the juice. The liquid thus obtained forms the basis of the wine and the pulp is discarded. Dissolve the sugar and acid in the elderberry "juice", and make the volume up to just under the gallon. When cool, add the enzyme and a yeast starter and pour into a demijohn. Fit an air-lock and ferment to dryness; rack and sweeten to taste in the normal way.

Notes

- The elderberries most suitable for winemaking are those which have little flavour of their own. It is therefore a good idea to taste the berries before you pick them, to check that their flavour is not too harsh or strong.

- The method of preparation described here avoids the extraction of too much tannin from the berries and so reduces the time required in store before the wine can be drunk. If pulp fermentation is preferred, the smoothness of the wine can be improved by adding the liquid obtained by simmering 1 lb (450 g) of chopped sultanas or peeled, sliced bananas in 2 pints (1.2 litres) of water for fifteen minutes.

- With a pulp fermentation, the sugar may be increased to 2½ lb/1.15 kg (USA 2 lb).

(3) ELDERBERRY DESSERT WINE

	British	Metric	USA
Fresh elderberries	3 lb	1.35 kg	2½ lb
Damsons or sloes	1 lb	450 g	12 oz
Ripe bananas	1 lb	450 g	12 oz
Sultanas or raisins	8 oz	225 g	6 oz
Sugar	3 lb	1.35 kg	2½ lb
Tartaric acid	3 tsp	3 tsp	3 tsp
Pectic enzyme			
Yeast and nutrient			
Water to	1 gallon	4.5 litres	1 gallon

Peel and slice the bananas and chop the sultanas. Boil both these fruits with the elderberries and damsons for 5 minutes only in 6 pints (3.5 litres) of water before transferring the whole mass to a fermentation bin. Add the acid and half the sugar and stir well to dissolve. When cool add the enzyme and a vigorous yeast starter. Ferment on pulp for 4 days, keeping well covered and stirring twice daily. Strain out the solids, pressing the pulp lightly to extract as much liquid as possible. Stir in half the remaining sugar, ensuring that it dissolves completely, and transfer the wine to a demijohn. Fit an air-lock and ferment for two weeks, after which add the rest of the sugar in 4-oz (110 g) lots every two or three weeks until fermentation has ended or the required degree of sweetness and strength has been achieved. Rack in normal way; store for nine months before bottling if possible, and a total of at least eighteen months to two years before drinking.

ELDERFLOWER WINE

(See also Elderflower "Champagne", page 180.)

	British	Metric	USA
Cream or white elderflowers (lightly pressed down)	1 pint	550 ml	1 pint

or Dried elderflowers	1 oz	30 g	1 oz
Concentrated white grape juice	½ pint	300 ml	½ pint
Sugar	1¾ lb	800 g	1½ lb
Citric acid	2 tsp	2 tsp	2 tsp
Grape tannin	¼ tsp	¼ tsp	¼ tsp
Yeast and nutrient			
Water to	1 gallon	4.5 litres	1 gallon

Pick the flowers on a dry day from a clean place nowhere near a road or suchlike. Trim off as many of the stems as possible. (This may be done by cutting off the flowers with scissors or by combing the florets off the stalks.) Place the florets in a fermentation bin and pour on 5 pints (2.8 litres) of water containing one dissolved Campden tablet. Leave covered for 24 hours, then dissolve the concentrate and sugar in 1 pint (600 ml) of water and add the solution to the flowers and water. Add the acid and tannin to the must, introduce a yeast starter and mix well. Ferment on "pulp" for 3 days, then strain into a demijohn, top up if necessary, fit an air-lock and ferment out to dryness. When racked and stabilized, the wine may be sweetened to taste. Ready to drink two or three months after final racking.

FRUIT JUICE WINES

Pure, unsweetened fruit juice in bottles and cartons has become very popular in recent years. This juice is ideal for winemaking because it provides all the flavour of the fruit with no difficulty of extraction or sterilization. Apple juice is filtered and beautifully clear, so there is no problem of unwanted sediment in the wine. And although orange, grapefruit and pineapple juice do contain some sediment, this settles out very easily and quickly after fermentation is complete to give a glorious golden-coloured wine. The flavour of the wine obviously depends on how much juice you use for each batch of wine. Too much juice can impart an excessively strong flavour to a wine, so don't exceed the quantities in the recipes, at least to start with. Here are some suggestions.

For 1 gallon (4.5 litres) of wine:

	British	Metric	USA
Unsweetened fruit juice (orange or pineapple or grapefruit or apple)	2–3 pints	1.2–1.7 litres	2–3 pints
Sugar	2¼ lb	1 kg	1¾ lb
Tannin	¼ tsp	¼ tsp	¼ tsp
Pectic enzyme			
Yeast and nutrient			
Water to	1 gallon	4.5 litres	1 gallon

Pour the fruit juice into the demijohn and add the tannin and sugar dissolved in water, ensuring that the contents of the demijohn are at the correct fermentation temperature. Add a yeast starter which has been prepared beforehand, and make the volume up to 1 gallon (4.5 litres). Ferment out under air lock, rack and bottle after fermentation is complete. The wine is then ready for drinking, and may be sweetened to taste. Serve chilled.

Notes

- Try to obtain unsweetened juices. If the ones you use do have sugar added, it may be wise to use a hydrometer to calculate the amount of sugar already present in the juice.
- Yeast nutrient and vitamin B tablets are essential. If you have no vitamin B, boil 6 oz (180 g) of liquid malt extract in water for three minutes and add it to the must. It will not affect the taste, but it will help the yeast to effect a vigorous fermentation.
- Most fruit juices in cartons will have the words "Made from concentrated fruit juice" on the container. However this does not mean that the juice is concentrated. If you wish to use concentrated fruit juices for winemaking, about 1–1½ pints (550–850 ml) should be enough for each gallon (4.5 litres) of wine.
- Try to obtain juices which specifically state that they contain no artificial preservative.

Other suggested recipes:

Orange and grapefruit: use 1 pint (550 ml) of orange juice and 1½ pints (850 ml) grapefruit juice in the above recipe.

Orange and pineapple: use 2 pints (1.2 litres) of orange juice and 1 pint (550 ml) of pineapple juice in the above recipe.

Orange and grape: a superb wine can be made by adding 1½ pints (850 ml) of orange juice to a can of white grape concentrate and making up to 1 gallon (4.5 litres) in the normal way.

GINGER WINE

Ginger wine is a delicious warming drink, traditionally for winter use — especially at Christmas. It is good on its own, even better with whisky as "Whisky Mac", and very simple to make.

	British	Metric	USA
Concentrated white grape juice	⅔ pint	400 ml	⅔ pint
Root ginger	3 oz	85 g	3 oz
Sugar	2 lb	900 g	1¾ lb
3 oranges			
Citric acid	½ tsp	½ tsp	½ tsp
Yeast and nutrient			
Water to	1 gallon	4.5 litres	1 gallon

Bruise the ginger and boil it in 3 pints (1.7 litres) of water together with the thinly pared peel of one orange for 20 minutes. Be very careful not to include any white pith, because it has a very strong bitter taste. Strain the liquid onto half the sugar and the juice of the oranges, stir to dissolve and allow to cool. Add the grape concentrate and mix well, then make up to just under the gallon (4.5 litres), leaving room for the remainder of the sugar. Fit an air-lock and ferment for three weeks. Then dissolve the remainder of the sugar in the wine, mix well, refit the air-lock and ferment to completion. Rack when the wine begins to clear, and, if you want "green ginger wine", add some green food colouring. Stabilize the wine, rack again when perfectly clear and store for 6 months before use.

GOOSEBERRY WINE

	British	Metric	USA
Green gooseberries, not quite ripe	4 lb	1.8 kg	3½ lb
Sugar	2½ lb	1.15 kg	2 lb
Citric acid	1½ tsp	1½ tsp	1½ tsp
Yeast and nutrient			
Pectic enzyme			
Water to	1 gallon	4.5 litres	1 gallon

One of the best country-fruit wines. Top and tail the gooseberries, wash them in cold water and place them in a fermentation bin or bucket. Dissolve 1 lb (450 g) of the sugar in 5 pints (2.8 litres) of boiling water and pour this over the fruit. Crush the berries, cover and leave to cool. Then add the acid, tannin, pectic enzyme and a yeast starter and stir well. Ferment on the pulp for 6 days, keeping well covered and stirring twice daily. Strain into a demijohn, dissolve the remainder of the sugar in enough water to bring the volume up to 1 gallon (4.5 litres), fit an air-lock and ferment to dryness. Rack as normal.

GOOSEBERRY AND LIME WINE

Add the thinly pared rind and juice of 5 limes to the gooseberries at the start of the pulp fermentation in the recipe above, but omit the citric acid.

GRAPE WINE
(1) Concentrated Grape Wine

Concentrated grape juice is both a useful additive to country wines which might otherwise lack a true wine character and a source of good quality home-made wine in its own right. Some winemakers use nothing but grape concentrates because they avoid the preparation of fruit and the "cookery" aspect of pulp fermentations or hot water extraction. Other winemakers use these concentrates because they provide an opportunity to make their favourite type of commercial wine at a fraction of the normal cost per bottle. The instructions will always be included with grape juice concentrates, so I need not repeat them here; it is, however, worthwhile pointing out that the finished wine benefits from storage in the same way as commercially made wine. I once kept a bottle of red wine made from one of the cheaper kits for four years, and the quality of the wine was remarkable. However, a general rule of thumb would be one year for whites and up to two years for reds. The obvious exceptions, of course, are the so-called "three-week wine" kits. If you're impatient, or in a hurry, try these; but don't expect the results to be as good as they would with the extra ingredients of patience and time!

(2) Fresh Grape Wine

Whether you have grown the grapes yourself or bought them, making wine from them can be an extravagant operation. Each gallon (4.5 litres) of wine will require about 12 lb (5.5 kg) of grapes. The method, however, is simple enough, and the results well worthwhile.

Fruit preparation: Red or White Grapes

Wash the grapes and remove the main stems. Then place them in a press or stout bag and press to extract the juice. Do not crush the pips. Run off the juice into demijohns for measurement — it should not be diluted — and check whether any extra sugar is required. The S.G. should be around 1.090 for a table wine and 1.115 for a strong sweet wine. Extra sugar may be necessary to achieve the appropriate gravity, especially if the grapes have been grown in an English summer! After calculating the amount of sugar required, return the juice to the pulp in a fermentation bin and dissolve 2 crushed Campden tablets per gallon (4.5 litres) of must, together with pectic enzyme. Cover and leave for 24 hours, stirring twice during that period.

RED GRAPES . . .

. . . are pulp fermented so that the colour and tannin in the skin and pips is leached out into the wine. After 24 hours have elapsed (see above), any extra sugar required is stirred into the must and a vigorous yeast starter is added. Pulp fermentation proceeds for about 8 days or until the wine is dark enough in colour. It is absolutely essential to submerge the cap of skins and pulp several times daily (using a wooden or stainless-steel spoon) to prevent acetification, i.e. to prevent bacteria settling on the pulp and turning the wine to vinegar. Alternatively, a heavy wooden board with several holes drilled in it can be floated on the surface of the wine to keep the pulp submerged. In any event, keep the must well covered and stir daily. At the end of this period, strain the wine into the demijohn(s), pressing the pulp to extract the maximum amount of liquid, fit an air-lock and ferment to dryness. Rack as normal, and when fermentation has ended and wine is absolutely clear, sweeten slightly if desired before placing in a demijohn for twelve months' storage.

WHITE GRAPES . . .

. . . obviously produce white wines, but a pulp fermentation is still desirable to add body and bouquet. Follow the procedure as described above, but ferment on the pulp for only 2 days. Finish the fermentation in a demijohn under air-lock. Rack as normal when the wine is clear. If possible, store for six months in a demijohn before bottling, and keep for another three months before use.

Notes

- The colour of red wines is derived from the skin of the grape, not the juice. So in theory the expressed juice of lightly pressed red grapes could be fermented directly to produce a white wine.
- If you aim to make a strong and sweet wine, remember to add the sugar in 4-oz (110 g) lots until the desired degree of strength and sweetness is obtained.
- Always protect the red wine from sunlight or the colour will fade. (See note on page 113.)

- If possible, check and adjust the acidity.
- See also Pyment, page 144.

GRAPEFRUIT WINE

	British	Metric	USA
Large grapefruit	6	6	6
Concentrated white grape juice	½ pint	300 ml	½ pint
Sugar	2 lb	900 g	1¾ lb
Grape tannin	¼ tsp	¼ tsp	¼ tsp
Yeast and nutrient			
Water to	1 gallon	4.5 litres	1 gallon

Press out the juice from the grapefruit and pour it into a demijohn. Thinly pare the rind from the fruit, being very careful to avoid all the white pith, as it imparts a very bitter taste to the wine. Place the rind in a small, sterile cloth or nylon mesh bag which can be suspended inside the demijohn. Dissolve half the sugar and the concentrate in 4 pints (2.3 litres) of water, add the tannin and transfer to the demijohn. Add a yeast starter and make the total volume up to about 7 pints (4 litres). Suspend the bag of rind in the wine, fit an air-lock and ferment for 7 days. Then remove the rinds, stir in the remainder of the sugar, top up to 1 gallon (4.5 litres) and refit air-lock. Ferment to dryness, rack and allow to clear before sweetening to taste. Ready to drink after three months.

See also Fruit Juice Wines, page 133-36.

GREENGAGE WINE

	British	Metric	USA
Ripe, stoned greengages	5 lb	2.3 kg	4 lb
Concentrated white grape juice	9 oz	250 g	⅓ pint
Sugar	2½ lb	1.15 kg	2 lb
Citric acid	1 tsp	1 tsp	1 tsp

Grape tannin	¼ tsp	¼ tsp	¼ tsp
Pectic enzyme			
Yeast and nutrient			
Water to	1 gallon	4.5 litres	1 gallon

Wash the fruit and crush it in a fermentation bin or bucket. Pour 5 pints (2.8 litres) of boiling water over it, cover and leave to cool. Dissolve 1 lb (450 g) of the sugar in 1 pint (550 ml) of hot water, allow to cool and add to the fruit. Add the concentrate, acid, tannin and enzyme, together with a yeast starter. Cover and ferment on pulp for 5 days, keeping well covered and stirring twice daily. Strain the liquid from the solids, but do not squeeze the pulp too hard or the fruit will become puréed. Stir the remainder of the sugar into the wine and top up with cooled boiled water if necessary. Fit an air-lock and ferment out in normal way. If possible store for three months in demijohn and another three months in bottle before use.

LEMON WINE

	British	Metric	USA
Pure, unsweetened lemon juice (e.g. PLJ)	12 fl oz	350 ml	12 fl oz
Thinly pared rind of 4 lemons			
Concentrated white grape juice	⅔ pint	400 ml	⅔ pint
Sugar	1¾ lb	800 g	1½ lb
Grape tannin	¼ tsp	¼ tsp	¼ tsp
Yeast and nutrient			
Water to	1 gallon	4.5 litres	1 gallon

Dissolve the sugar, grape concentrate and tannin in 4 pints (2.3 litres) of water and mix with the lemon juice in a demijohn. Add a yeast starter and make the total volume up to the gallon (4.5 litres). Place the thinly pared rind of the lemons in a small sterile cloth or nylon mesh bag and suspend it in the demijohn for 7 days. Fit an air-lock and ferment to dryness. Allow the wine to clear and rack in the normal way. If the wine is too acid, the acidity may be masked by adding a little sugar syrup or glycerine — say 4 fl oz (100 ml). Alternatively the acidity may be reduced with a proprietary "Wine Acid Reduction Solution" or, preferably, potassium carbonate (see page 89). This wine will be ready three months after fermentation has finished and is ideal to serve cold on a hot summer's day.

LIME WINE

(By Bath Wine Circle)

	British	Metric	USA
Rose's Lime Juice	½ bottle [12 fl oz]	350 ml	12 fl oz
Bananas	1 lb	450 g	1 lb
Minced sultanas	8 oz	225 g	8oz
Sugar	2½ lb	1.15 kg	2 lb
Pectic enzyme			
Yeast and nutrient			
Water to	1 gallon	4.5 litres	1 gallon

Peel the bananas and chop finely. Bring 1 gallon (4.5 litres) of water to the boil, add the chopped bananas and boil for ¾ hour. Place sultanas and sugar in plastic bin. Strain the liquid from the bananas onto the sugar and stir well to dissolve. When cool add lime juice, nutrient and yeast starter. Allow to ferment for 3 days then strain into gallon jar (4.5 litres) and fit air-lock. Rack as necessary. This is generally a very quick wine to produce.

MAIZE WINE

	British	Metric	USA
Crushed maize	2 lb	900 g	2 lb
Sugar	2¾ lb	1.25 kg	2¼ lb
Sultanas or raisins	1 lb	450 g	12 oz

Citric acid	2 tsp	2 tsp	2 tsp
Grape tannin	¼ tsp	¼ tsp	¼ tsp
Pectic enzyme			
Fungal amylase or diastase			
Yeast and nutrient			
Water to	1 gallon	4.5 litres	1 gallon

You can buy crushed maize at health food or winemaking suppliers. Wash and chop the sultanas, and place them together with the maize flakes in a fermentation bin or bucket. Pour on 6 pints (3.5 litres) of cold water containing two dissolved Campden tablets and leave for 24 hours. Then add the remainder of the ingredients and make up to 1 gallon (4.5 litres). Ferment on pulp for 3 days, keeping well covered and stirring twice daily. Strain into a demijohn, top up if necessary with cool boiled water, fit an air-lock and ferment out. If the wine is wanted strong and sweet, add an extra 8 oz (2.25 g) of sugar in 2-oz (60g) lots at two-weekly intervals just before fermentation has finished, until the desired strength and sweetness is obtained. See the note on cereal wines at the end of the recipe for Barley Wine, page 112.

MEAD, MELOMEL AND METHEGLIN

(1) MEAD

Mead is made from a solution of honey in water which is fermented in the normal way. This is possible because honey is really nothing more than a very concentrated sugar solution produced as food by bees from the pollen and nectar of flowers. The flavour and bouquet of honey, and in turn of mead, thus depend on the flowers visited by the bees. Strongly scented honey such as lilac, or cheap imported honey containing, say, eucalyptus scent is unsuitable. The best meads are made from orange blossom and clover honey. Although mead is a drink distinctly different to wine, and not to everyone's taste, it is worthwhile trying at least one batch for fun. The fruit flavoured varieties, especially pyment, are particularly attractive drinks once you have developed a taste for mead. Before you buy any honey, check the ingredients to ensure that it is "Pure" and unadulterated.

Honey contains little acid or nutrient, and it is important that enough is added or the fermentation will be impossibly slow or even incomplete. A double dose of nutrient and vitamin B, or a double dose of a ready vitaminized nutrient such as *Tronozymol* is essential. In addition, honey is far from sterile and must be sterilized before it is used. This is done by heating it in water to boiling point. The recipe below is for a basic Mead.

	British	Metric	USA
Honey	3 lb	1.35 kg	2½ lb
Tartaric. acid	1½ tsp	1½ tsp	1½ tsp
Citric acid	1½ tsp	1½ tsp	1½ tsp
Nutrient and vitamins	See text above		
Grape tannin	¼ tsp	¼ tsp	¼ tsp
Yeast			
Water to	1 gallon	4.5 litres	1 gallon

Prepare a yeast starter 24 hours before compounding the must. Dissolve the honey in 5 pints (2.8 litres) of water and heat to boiling point, stirring continuously. Skim off any scum, then allow to cool. At 25°C (77°F) add the acid, tannin and yeast starter. Mix well and transfer to a demijohn. Top up to 1 gallon (4.5 litres), fit an air-lock and ferment out. Rack as normal and allow to mature for at least three months before use. However, the full enjoyment of mead can only be obtained if it is stored for a year or more — even up to three years for strongly scented honey. The mead is better at least slightly sweet when served, so use a little sugar syrup (4 oz or 110 g dissolved in the minimum quantity of water) to sweeten to taste after the final racking.

MELOMEL

Melomel is the name given to fruit flavoured mead. Traditionally, melomel is flavoured with blackcurrants, although rosehips are equally suitable. Other possibilities include orange, lemon, apple and grape juice (particularly good).

BLACKCURRANT OR ROSEHIP MELOMEL

Follow the basic recipe for mead, but add 12 fl oz (350 ml) of rosehip or blackcurrant syrup. Note: if the syrup contains preservative, boil it in a little water for 2 minutes to drive it off, otherwise the yeast will be prevented from working.

ORANGE OR LEMON

Follow the basic recipe for mead, but add the juice of 5 oranges or lemons to the mixture and suspend a small sterile cloth or nylon mesh bag containing the thinly pared rind of two of the fruits in the fermenting must until the desired strength of flavour has been achieved. In addition, cut the acid by half when using oranges, and omit it altogether when using lemons.

APPLE (CYSER)

Follow the basic recipe for mead, but add 1½ pints (850 ml) of unsweetened apple juice to the honey.

GRAPE (PYMENT)

Use 2 lb (900 g) of honey and 1 pint (550 ml) of concentrated white grape juice in the basic mead recipe.

METHEGLIN

Follow the recipe for mead, but suspend a small, fine-mesh nylon or cloth bag containing the contents of 1 small packet of dried mixed herbs *or* spices (available from most winemaking specialists) in the must for two or three weeks at the start of fermentation. Remove it when the flavour is strong enough for your taste.

MINT WINE

There are several varieties of mint commonly grown in gardens: the common garden mint, peppermint and spearmint are all suitable for making wine.

	British	Metric	USA
Concentrated white grape juice	1 can (for 1 gallon/4.5 litres of wine)		
Young fresh mint leaves	1½ pints	850 ml	
Sugar	As instructed on concentrate can		
Yeast and nutrient			
Water to	1 gallon	4.5 litres	1 gallon

Make up the grape concentrate as instructed on the can, but instead of pouring straight into a demijohn, ferment in a bucket with the mint leaves for 3 or 4 days. Then strain into a demijohn, fit an air-lock and proceed as normal. Alternatively, oil of mint (if you can get it) may be dissolved in the finished wine a little at a time until the desired strength of flavour is obtained.

MIXED DRIED FRUIT WINE

	British	Metric	USA
Mixed dried fruit (raisins, currants, sultanas)	2 lb	900 g	1¾ lb
Sugar	1½ lb	700 g	1½ lb
Citric acid	2 tsp	2 tsp	2 tsp
Grape tannin	⅛ tsp	⅛ tsp	⅛ tsp
Pectic enzyme			
Yeast and nutrient			
Water to	1 gallon	4.5 litres	1 gallon

Wash and drain the fruit, then chop or mince it and place it in a fermentation bin or bucket. Pour 6 pints (3.5 litres) of boiling water over the fruit, cover and leave to cool. When at correct fermentation temperature, add the acid, tannin and pectic enzyme, together with a vigorous yeast starter. Ferment on the pulp for 7 days, keeping well covered and stirring twice daily. Strain the liquid onto the sugar, pressing the pulp gently to extract the maximum volume of liquid. Stir well to dissolve the sugar and transfer to a demijohn. Top up with water to 1 gallon (4.5 litres) if necessary and fit an air-lock. Ferment to dryness, rack in normal way and sweeten to taste. Ready to drink after six months but improves with keeping for one year. A surprisingly good wine.

MIXED FRESH FRUIT WINE

	British	Metric	USA
Mixed summer fruits*	4 lb	1.8 kg	4 lb
Sugar	2 lb	900 g	1¾ lb
Pure unsweetened apple juice	1 pint	550 ml	1 pint
Citric acid	1 tsp	1 tsp	1 tsp
Grape tannin	¼ tsp	¼ tsp	¼ tsp
Pectic enzyme			
Yeast and nutrient			
Water to	1 gallon	4.5 litres	1 gallon

*Use a mixture of several "white" or pink summer fruits such as strawberries, redcurrants, gooseberries, greengage, yellow plums, peaches and so on. This produces a delicious wine of very good quality.

Wash the fruit and remove all stalks, leaves and stones. Place it in a fermentation bin, add 5 pints (2.8 litres) of cold water containing 2 dissolved Campden tablets, mash the fruit, cover and leave for 24 hours. Then add the apple juice and a vigorously fermenting yeast starter and pectic enzyme. Stir well; ferment on pulp for 5 days, keeping well covered and stirring twice daily. Strain and press the fruit, dissolve the sugar in the liquid and transfer to a demijohn. Top up if necessary, fit an air-lock and ferment out to dryness. Rack and sweeten to taste when wine is perfectly clear.

146

Note

- If you have a hydrometer and pH papers, it is a good idea to check both the sugar content of the must and the acidity. (The S.G. of the full volume of must should be about 1.090; the acidity pH 3.3.) This will enable you to adjust the amount of sugar and citric acid in the recipe to take account of any variations in the ripeness of the different fruits.

MIXED TINNED FRUIT WINE
(By Bath Wine Circle)

	British	*Metric*	*USA*
Tinned fruit	2 × 15½ oz cans	2 × 450 g cans	2 lb
Sugar	2½ lb	1.15 kg	2 lb
Peeled bananas	2	2	2
Washed, minced raisins or sultanas	8 oz	225 g	8 oz
Citric acid	1 tsp	1 tsp	1 tsp
Grape tannin	⅛ tsp	⅛ tsp	⅛ tsp
Yeast and nutrient			
Water to	1 gallon	4.5 litres	1 gallon

Dissolve the sugar in 1½ pints (850 ml) of boiling water and add the contents of two 15½ oz (450 g) cans of fruit, 2 bananas (chopped thinly) and the minced raisins or sultanas. Pour on 5½ pints (3.1 litres) of boiling water, then add the citric acid and grape tannin. When all is cool, (24°C/75°F) add the contents of a starter bottle of prepared wine yeast. Cover closely and allow to ferment in a warm place for five days. Strain into a gallon (4.5 litres) jar and fit an air-lock. Rack as necessary.

MORELLO CHERRY WINE

As for Cherry Wine, pages 121-2. Best as a strong, sweet dessert wine.

NECTARINE WINE

As for Peach Wine, page 151-2.

ORANGE WINE

	British	Metric	USA
Sweet oranges	10 or 12	10 or 12	10
Raisins or sultanas	12 oz	350 g	8 oz
Sugar	2½ lb	1.15 kg	2 lb
Citric acid	½ tsp	½ tsp	½ tsp
Grape tannin	⅛ tsp	⅛ tsp	⅛ tsp
Pectic enzyme			
Yeast and nutrient			
Water to	1 gallon	4.5 litres	1 gallon

Thinly pare the rind from six of the oranges, ensuring that you avoid all the white pith, which can impart a very bitter taste to the wine. Set the rind to one side. Squeeze out the juice of the oranges and add it to the washed, chopped raisins or sultanas in a fermentation bin or bucket. Dissolve the sugar in 6 pints (3.5 litres) of boiling water and pour the solution over the raisins. When cool, add the rind, acid, tannin, pectic enzyme and a yeast starter. Cover and leave to ferment for 5 days, stirring twice daily. Strain the liquid into a demijohn, squeezing the pulp gently to extract the maximum amount of liquid. Top up with water if necessary, fit an air-lock and ferment to dryness. Rack when fermentation has finished and wine begins to clear, and again when it is "star bright". Ready to drink after three months, although it is best after six to nine months.

See also Seville Orange Wine, pages 166-7; Fruit Juice Wines, pages 133-5.

ORANGE AND ROSEHIP WINE

A delicious wine can be produced by adding one 12 fl oz (350 ml) bottle of rosehip syrup to any orange wine recipe.

ORANGE BLOSSOM WINE

	British	Metric	USA
Dried orange blossom, 1 packet	2 oz	50 g	2 oz
Concentrated white grape juice	⅔ pint	400 ml	⅔ pint
Sugar	1¾ lb	800 g	1½ lb
Citric acid	1 tsp	1 tsp	1 tsp
Grape tannin	⅛ tsp	⅛ tsp	⅛ tsp
Yeast and nutrient			
Pectic enzyme			
Water to	1 gallon	4.5 litres	1 gallon

Carefully remove all foreign matter such as twigs, stones and so on from the flowers and place the petals in a bucket containing 5 pints (2.8 litres) of cold water in which a Campden tablet has been dissolved. Then proceed as for Elderflower Wine, page 132.

PARSNIP WINE

	British	Metric	USA
Parsnips	5 lb	2.3 kg	4 lb
Concentrated white grape juice	9 oz	250 g	⅓ pint
Sugar	2¼ lb	1 kg	1¾ lb
Citric acid	2 tsp	2 tsp	2 tsp
Grape tannin	¼ tsp	¼ tsp	¼ tsp
Pectic enzyme			
Fungal amylase			
Yeast and nutrient			
Water to	1 gallon	4.5 litres	1 gallon

Scrub the parsnips clean but do not peel them. Cut them into chunks and boil the pieces in unsalted water until they are tender but not mushy. Then strain off the liquid, being careful not to squeeze the parsnip pieces. To the liquid, add the concentrate, sugar, acid and tannin. Stir well to dissolve and allow to cool. Then mix in the enzymes, yeast and nutrient and top up to 1 gallon (4.5 litres). Transfer to demijohn, fit an air-lock and proceed as normal. An excellent wine, best after a year or more's maturation. Good dry, even better strong and sweet.

PEACH TABLE WINE (1)

A superb home-made wine, well worth making in quantity.

	British	Metric	USA
Fresh, ripe peaches	4½ lb	2 kg	4 lb
Ripe bananas	3	3	3
Sugar	2½ lb	1.15 kg	2 lb
Citric acid	1 tsp	1 tsp	1 tsp
Grape tannin	¼ tsp	¼ tsp	¼ tsp
Pectic enzyme			
Yeast and nutrient			
Water to	1 gallon	4.5 litres	1 gallon

Wash the peaches but do not peel them. Chop, remove the stones and place in a fermentation bin or bucket with the peeled, sliced bananas. Dissolve 1 lb (450 g) of the sugar in 6 pints of boiling water and pour over the fruit. Cover and leave to cool. At correct temperature, add the enzyme, acid, tannin and a yeast starter, stir well and cover. Ferment on pulp for 4 days, keeping well covered and stirring twice daily. Strain into a demijohn and add the remainder of the sugar dissolved in enough water to bring the volume up to 1 gallon (4.5 litres). Fit an air-lock and ferment out. Rack as normal, and when certain that the ferment is complete and the wine is stable, sweeten very slightly to produce a medium dry wine. Store for six months (if you can wait!) before use.

Note

• Unripe peaches do not make good wine.

150

PEACH TABLE WINE (2)

	British	Metric	USA
Canned peaches	3 × 15½-oz cans	3 × 450 g cans	3 lb
Ripe bananas	3	3	3
Sugar	2¼ lb	1 kg	1¾ lb
Citric acid	2 tsp	2 tsp	2 tsp
Grape tannin	⅛ tsp	⅛ tsp	⅛ tsp
Pectic enzyme			
Yeast and nutrient			
Water to	1 gallon	4.5 litres	1 gallon

Place the fruit and syrup in a bucket with the peeled, sliced bananas. Dissolve 1 lb (450 g) of the sugar in 6 pints (3.5 litres) of boiling water and pour over the fruit. Mash well. Cover and leave to cool. Then proceed as for Peach Wine (1).

Note

• Dried peaches (1½ lb/700 g) may be used in this recipe, but should be boiled in the water for 5 minutes before being placed in the fermenting bin.

PEACH DESSERT WINE

	British	Metric	USA
Fresh, ripe peaches	4½ lb	2 kg	4 lb
Bananas	1 lb	450 g	12 oz
Concentrated white grape juice	¾ pint	425 ml	¾ pint
Sugar	2¼ lb	1 kg	1¾ lb
Glycerol	1½ fl oz	40 ml	1 fl oz
Citric acid	2 tsp	2 tsp	2 tsp
Grape tannin	½ tsp	½ tsp	½ tsp
Pectic enzyme			
Yeast and nutrient			

| Water to | 1 gallon | 4.5 litres | 1 gallon |

Wash, chop and remove the stones from the peaches. Place in a fermentation bin with the peeled, sliced bananas and add 5 pints (2.8 litres) of boiling water in which 1 lb (450 g) of sugar has been dissolved. Crush the fruit, cover and leave to cool. Add the concentrate, glycerol, acid, tannin and enzyme, together with a yeast starter. Ferment on pulp for 5 days, keeping well covered and stirring twice daily. Strain into a demijohn, fit air-lock and ferment for four weeks. Then add the remainder of the sugar in 4-oz (110 g) lots every two or three weeks until the desired degree of strength and sweetness has been achieved. Rack as normal, and store for two years before use.

PEACH AND REDCURRANT WINE

Follow the recipes for Peach Wine, but add 2 lb (900 g) of redcurrants to the pulp fermentation. (If possible, check the acidity and adjust as necessary.)

PEAPOD WINE

Although an extraordinary base, peapods really can produce a wine of very good quality.

	British	Metric	USA
Peapods (without the peas!)	4 lb	1.8 kg	3½ lb
Concentrated white grape juice	½ pint	300 ml	½ pint
Sugar	2 lb	900 g	1¾ lb
Citric acid	1½ tsp	1½ tsp	1½ tsp
Grape tannin	½ tsp	½ tsp	½ tsp
Yeast and nutrient			
Water to	1 gallon	4.5 litres	1 gallon

Wash the peapods, chop them and boil in 5 pints (2.8 litres) of water until they are tender but not pulpy. Strain off the liquid, and add the sugar and concentrate. Stir well to dissolve. When the solution has cooled, add the other ingredients and a yeast starter. Transfer to a demijohn, top up with water if necessary to

1 gallon (4.5 litres), fit an air-lock and ferment to dryness. Rack in normal way; the wine needs only a few months' storage, and is excellent as a light dry or medium-dry table wine.

PEAR WINE (1)

	British	Metric	USA
Fresh pears	5 lb	2.3 kg	4 lb
or Canned pears	4 × 15½ oz cans	4 × 450 g cans	4 lb
Concentrated white grape juice	9 oz	250 g	⅓ pint
Sugar	2¼ lb	1 kg	1¾ lb
Citric acid	2 tsp	2 tsp	2 tsp
Grape tannin*	½ tsp	½ tsp	½ tsp
Pectic enzyme			
Yeast and nutrient			
Water to	1 gallon	4.5 litres	1 gallon

*omit the tannin if using unpeeled fresh pears.

If the pears are hard, peel and cut them into chunks, avoiding the core. Drop the chunks into 5 pints (2.8 litres) of water and boil until they are soft. Then transfer the fruit and liquid to the fermentation bin. *If the pears are soft*, clean them (do not peel) and mash in a fermentation bin before adding 5 pints (2.8 litres) of boiling water. Allow to cool. Then: Add the enzyme, tannin, acid, grape concentrate and half the sugar dissolved in 1 pint (600 ml) of water at fermentation temperature. Introduce a yeast starter, cover and leave to ferment for 5 days, stirring twice daily. Then strain into a demijohn, pressing the fruit gently to extract the liquid. Add the remaining sugar dissolved in enough water to top up to the gallon (4.5 litres), fit an air-lock and ferment to dryness. Rack in normal way, and store for three months before bottling. Ready to drink after six months.

Note
- Dessert pears are not as satisfactory as the "cooking" varieties.

153

PEAR WINE (2)

(By Alan Middleton, Abbey Park and Leicester Circle Show Winner)

	British	Metric	USA
Small ripe pears	6 lb	2.7 kg	5 lb
Raisins	4 oz	110 g	4 oz
Sugar	2½ lb	1.15 kg	2 lb
Jif lemon juice	4 tsp	4 tsp	4 tsp
Grape tannin solution	10 drops	10 drops	10 drops
Pectic enzyme			
Yeast and nutrient			
Water to	1 gallon	4.5 litres	1 gallon

Cut pears into small pieces, chop raisins and put in a bucket. Pour over 6 pints (3.5 litres) of boiling water, add sugar. Leave to cool, add yeast, nutrient, juice and enzyme. Leave in bucket for 2 days, stirring twice daily. Strain into demijohn and ferment out in usual way.

PEAR AND FIG WINE

	British	Metric	USA
Ripe pears	3 lb	1.35 kg	3 lb
Figs	1 lb	450 g	12 oz
or Dried figs	6 oz	170 g	4 oz
Sugar	2¼ lb	1 kg	1¾ lb
Citric acid	2 tsp	2 tsp	2 tsp
Pectic enzyme			
Yeast and nutrient			
Water to	1 gallon	4.5 litres	1 gallon

Chop up the whole pears and place in a fermentation bin with the figs. Pour on 6 pints (3.5 litres) of boiling water and mash gently. When cool, add the enzyme and acid, together with a vigorous yeast. Leave to ferment on pulp for 3 days, keeping well covered and stirring twice daily. Next strain through a coarse and then through a fine mesh straining bag or cloth onto the sugar, stir well to dissolve, and transfer to a demijohn. Top up to the gallon (4.5 litres) if necessary, fit an air-lock and ferment to dryness. Rack as necessary (this wine tends to throw a heavy deposit) and store for six months. The wine may be sweetened to taste; serve as a medium sweet wine for "social" drinking.

PEAR AND SLOE (OR DAMSON) WINE

	British	Metric	USA
Pears	4 lb	1.8 kg	4 lb
Fresh sloes	1½ lb	450 g	1 lb
or Dried sloes	8 oz	225 g	8 oz
or Fresh damsons	1½ lb	700 g	1½ lb
Sugar	2½ lb	1.15 kg	2 lb
Tartaric acid	2 tsp	2 tsp	2 tsp
Pectic enzyme			
Yeast and nutrient			
Water to	1 gallon	4.5 litres	1 gallon

Wash the red fruit and heat it in 6 pints (3.5 litres) of water at 80°C (180°F) for 15 minutes. Mash it, then strain through a nylon or cloth straining mesh onto the sugar. Squeeze gently and then discard the pulp. Stir the liquid well to dissolve the sugar, then pour over the peeled chopped pears in a fermentation bin. Allow to cool, then add all the other ingredients and make the total volume up to 1 gallon (4.5 litres). Cover and ferment on pulp for 3 days, keeping well covered and stirring twice daily. Then strain into a demijohn, top up if necessary, fit an air-lock and ferment to dryness. A very good light red wine which can be served about four months after the final racking.

Note
- This recipe is particularly useful for adding character to wine made from rather bland pears.

155

PINEAPPLE WINE (1)

	British	Metric	USA
Fresh pineapples (medium sized)	4	4	4
Sugar	2½ lb	1.15 kg	2 lb
Citric acid	1 tsp	1 tsp	1 tsp
Grape tannin	¼ tsp	¼ tsp	¼ tsp
Pectic enzyme			
Yeast and nutrient			
Water to	1 gallon	4.5 litres	1 gallon

Wash the pineapples and then remove their tops and bottoms. It is, however, not necessary to peel them. Simply cut them into medium-sized chunks and boil them in 6 pints (3.5 litres) of water for 5 minutes. Then transfer fruit and liquid to a fermenting bin, stir in the sugar, acid and tannin. Leave to cool then add the yeast. Cover and ferment on pulp for 3 days before straining into a demijohn. Top up if necessary, fit an air-lock and ferment out. Rack in the usual way; when the wine is quite stable it may be sweetened slightly if desired.

See also: Fruit Juice Wines, pages 133-5.

PINEAPPLE WINE (2)

	British	Metric	USA
Canned pineapple	4 × 15½ oz cans	4 × 450 g cans	4 lb
or Crystallized pineapple	2 lb	900 g	2 lb
Sugar	2 lb	900 g	1¾ lb
Citric acid	2 tsp	2 tsp	2 tsp
Grape tannin	⅓ tsp	⅓ tsp	⅓ tsp
Pectic enzyme			
Yeast and nutrient			
Water to	1 gallon	4.5 litres	1 gallon

Dissolve the sugar in 6 pints (3.5 litres) of boiling water and pour the solution over the chopped fruit and syrup in a fermentation bucket. Allow to cool, then add the other ingredients. Ferment on pulp for 5 days, keeping well covered and stirring twice daily. Strain into a demijohn, top up if necessary with cooled, boiled water and fit an air-lock. Leave to ferment out, then rack as usual.

PLUM WINE

	British	Metric	USA
Mixed red, golden or black plums	5 lb	2.3 kg	4 lb
Concentrated red grape juice	½ pint	300 ml	½ pint
Sugar	2 lb	900 g	1¾ lb
Tartaric acid	2 tsp	2 tsp	2 tsp
Pectic enzyme			
Yeast and nutrient			
Water to	1 gallon	4.5 litres	1 gallon

Wash the plums, cut them in half and remove the stones. Place in a fermentation bucket and crush the fruit well (this can be done by hand). Pour on 6 pints (3.5 litres) of boiling water in which half the sugar has been dissolved. Cover and leave to cool. Then add the pectic enzyme, acid and yeast. Ferment on pulp for 4 days, keeping well covered and stirring twice daily. Strain the liquid onto the remaining sugar, stir well to dissolve, transfer to a demijohn and top up with water if necessary. Ferment out to dryness, rack so that the wine is completely stable and store for six months before use.

Notes
- Canned plums may be used if desired.
- By adding ⅔ pint (400 ml) of concentrated red grape juice and feeding the sugar in stages, a very good dessert wine can be produced.

RAISIN WINE

Follow the recipes for Sultana Wine, pages 168-9, using raisins in place of sultanas. See also Mixed Dried Fruit Wine, page 145.

RASPBERRY AND GRAPE WINE

Raspberries do not make an outstanding wine, being too strongly flavoured and scented. However, one good way of using the fruit is to flavour a grape-concentrate wine. This can easily be done by making up one of the cheaper white grape concentrates as instructed on the can, but fermenting in a bucket with 2 lb (900 g) of raspberries for 4 days before straining into a demijohn.

RASPBERRY AND BANANA WINE

	British	Metric	USA
Fresh raspberries	3 lb	1.35 kg	2½ lb
Bananas, very ripe	2 lb	900 g	1½ lb
Sugar	2½ lb	1.15 kg	2 lb
Citric acid	1 tsp	1 tsp	1 tsp
Grape tannin	⅛ tsp	⅛ tsp	⅛ tsp
Pectic enzyme			
Yeast and nutrient			
Water to	1 gallon	4.5 litres	1 gallon

Peel and slice the bananas, and place them together with the washed raspberries in a fermentation bin or bucket. Dissolve the sugar in 7 pints (4 litres) of boiling water and pour it over the fruit. Allow to cool, then add the other ingredients. Pulp ferment for 4 days, then strain into a demijohn, top up if necessary, fit an air-lock and proceed as normal.

REDCURRANT WINE

	British	Metric	USA
Ripe redcurrants	3 lb	1.35 kg	2½ lb
Concentrated red grape juice	9 oz	250 g	⅓ pint
Sugar	2½ lb	1.15 kg	2 lb
Pectic enzyme			
Yeast and nutrient			
Water to	1 gallon	4.5 litres	1 gallon

Place the redcurrants in a fermentation bin and pour onto them 7 pints (4 litres) of boiling water in which the sugar has been dissolved. Allow to cool, then add all the other ingredients. Stir well; ferment on the pulp for 5 days before straining into a demijohn. Top up with cool boiled water if required, fit an air-lock and ferment out. Rack and stabilize before sweetening to taste. Store for at least three months before use.

RED TABLE WINE

The following are a selection of recipes producing red wines from a mixture of fruits which should be available in dried, fresh or canned form.

(1) BLACKBERRY, ELDERBERRY AND MALT

For 5 gallons (22.5 litres):	British	Metric	USA
Fresh, frozen or canned blackberries	15 lb	6.8 kg	12½ lb
Fresh elderberries	5 lb	2.3 kg	4 lb
or Dried elderberries	1½ lb	680 g	1½ lb
Liquid malt extract	2 lb	900 g	1½ lb
Sugar	11 lb	5 kg	9 lb
Tartaric acid	5 tsp	5 tsp	5 tsp
Pectic enzyme			

159

Yeast and nutrient

Water to	5 gallons	22.5 litres	5 gallons

These quantities may be scaled up or down for larger or smaller volumes of wine.

Wash the fruit and remove all foreign matter. Strip the elderberries from their stalks. Place all the fruit in a large bin or other fermentation vessel and pour on 3 gallons (15 litres) of boiling water in which the malt extract and half the sugar have been dissolved. Mash gently, cover and leave to cool. At fermentation temperature, add the acid, enzyme and a vigorous yeast starter. Ferment on the pulp for 4 days, keeping well covered and stirring twice daily. Strain into demijohns or other fermentation vessels and add the remaining sugar dissolved in enough water to make the volume up to 5 gallons (22.5 litres). Fit an air-lock and ferment out as normal. Rack and store for six to nine months, or longer if necessary, before use.

(2) DAMSON AND ELDERBERRY

For 5 gallons (22.5 litres):	British	Metric	USA
Fresh, ripe damsons	12 lb	5.4 kg	10 lb
Fresh elderberries	2 lb	900 g	2 lb
or Dried elderberries	10 oz	300 g	8 oz
Sultanas or raisins	2½ lb	1.15 kg	2 lb
Apple juice in carton or bottle	3 pints	1.7 litres	3 pints
Sugar	11 lb	5 kg	9 lb
Pectic enzyme			
Yeast and nutrient			
Water to	5 gallons	22.5 litres	5 gallons

Wash and crush the damsons and pour 2 gallons (9 litres) of boiling water over them. Next, heat the minced sultanas and the elderberries in 1 gallon (4.5 litres) of water to boiling point and simmer for 5 minutes. Then strain off the liquid, pressing the pulp gently, and add it to the damsons. Allow to cool and then add the enzyme, nutrient and apple juice and half the sugar as syrup. Stir, introduce a yeast starter and ferment on pulp for 1 day only. Then strain off into jars, add the remainder of the sugar dissolved in enough water to bring the volume up to 5 gallons (22.5 litres) and proceed as normal.

RHUBARB WINE

	British	Metric	USA
Red rhubarb stems picked in May or June	5 lb	2.3 kg	4 lb
Concentrated white grape juice	9 oz	250 g	1/3 pint
Sugar	2¼ lb	1 kg	1¾ lb
Lemons	4	4	4
Grape tannin	¼ tsp	¼ tsp	¼ tsp
Pectic enzyme			
Yeast and nutrient			
Water to	1 gallon	4.5 litres	1 gallon

Wash and chop the rhubarb stalks and crush them. Place the pieces in a fermentation bin, together with 5 pints (2.8 litres) of water containing a dissolved Campden tablet. Cover and leave for 24 hours before adding the remainder of the ingredients dissolved in 1 pint (600 ml) of cold water. Ferment on pulp for 3 days, keeping well covered and stirring twice daily. Strain off the solids, pressing the pulp gently, and place in a demijohn under an air-lock. Allow any foaming to die away, then top up to the gallon (4.5 litres) and ferment out in the normal way.

Notes

- Rhubarb is not an outstanding wine, and its main use tends to be for blending and so on. It has a delicate flavour and colour which is not too pronounced in a blend.
- Use only freshly picked stalks of rhubarb — the younger the better. Provided only young stalks are used, and no hot water is added, it is not necessary to use precipitated chalk to neutralize the oxalic acid in the rhubarb.
- Rhubarb *leaves* are poisonous.

161

RHUBARB, APPLE AND GRAPE WINE

	British	Metric	USA
Rhubarb	4 lb	1.8 kg	3½ lb
Pure apple juice	¾ pint	425 ml	¾ pint
Concentrated grape juice	½ pint	300 ml	½ pint
Sugar	2 lb	900 g	1¾ lb
Grape tannin	¼ tsp	¼ tsp	¼ tsp
Pectic enzyme			
Yeast and nutrient			
Water to	1 gallon	4.5 litres	1 gallon

Wash and slice the rhubarb thinly. Place in a fermentation bin and cover with the dry sugar. Leave for 24 hours so that most of the sugar dissolves in the rhubarb "juice". Strain off the syrup, washing the pulp with cool water to ensure all the sugar passes into the must. Add the remainder of the ingredients and stir to ensure that the sugar is completely dissolved before transferring to a demijohn and topping up to just under the gallon (4.5 litres). Fit an air-lock and ferment out in the normal way, topping up to the final volume when any foaming has died away. The wine is ready to drink soon after the second racking, but will improve with keeping up to about six months.

RICE WINE

Only the epidermis (the outer coat) of rice grains plays any part in contributing flavour to rice wine. Thus the "polished" white rice normally used for cooking is useless, since it consists of nothing but starch, which yeast cannot ferment and which forms a gelatinous suspension in the finished wine. However, un-polished or "brown" rice with the epidermis left on should be available from most good grocers, health food stores and winemaking suppliers. Brown rice is also known as paddy rice or husked rice.

	British	Metric	USA
Brown rice	3 lb	1.35 kg	2½ lb
Sultanas	8 oz	225 g	8 oz
Sugar	2½ lb	1.15 kg	2 lb
Grape tannin	¼ tsp	¼ tsp	¼ tsp
Pectic enzyme (if using raisins)			
Fungal amylase or diastase			
Yeast and nutrient			
Water to	1 gallon	4.5 litres	1 gallon

Method as for Barley Wine, pages 112.

RICE AND RAISIN WINE

One of the favourite wines of many home winemakers, and a very good one, too.

	British	Metric	USA
Brown rice	2 lb	900 g	1¾ lb
Raisins	2 lb	900 g	1¾ lb
Sugar	2¼ lb	1 kg	2 lb
Citric acid	2 tsp	2 tsp	2 tsp
Grape tannin	¼ tsp	¼ tsp	¼ tsp
Pectic enzyme			
Fungal amylase or diastase			
Yeast and nutrient			
Water to	1 gallon	4.5 litres	1 gallon

Wash and chop the raisins, place them in a fermentation bin with the washed rice grains, and pour on 6 pints (3.5 litres) of boiling water in which half the sugar has been dissolved. Cover and leave to cool. At 20°C (68°F) add the yeast, enzymes, acid and tannin. Ferment on pulp for 5 days, keeping well covered and stirring twice daily. Then strain off the liquid, transfer it to a demijohn, and add the remaining sugar dissolved in enough water to bring the volume up to the gallon (4.5 litres). Fit an air-lock and ferment out; rack in the normal way, and when the wine is stable, sweeten to taste, storing for at least three months before use.

ROSEHIP WINE (1)

	British	Metric	USA
Fresh rosehips	4 lb	1.8 kg	3½ lb
or Dried rosehip shells	1½ lb	700 g	1½ lb
Sugar	2½ lb	1.15 kg	2 lb
Citric acid	2 tsp	2 tsp	2 tsp
Grape tannin	¼ tsp	¼ tsp	¼ tsp
Pectic enzyme			
Yeast and nutrient			
Water to	1 gallon	4.5 litres	1 gallon

First wash the rosehips in cold water, removing as many stalks and flower heads as possible. Then simmer the whole hips in about 6 pints (3.5 litres) of boiling water for ten minutes or so. Add half the sugar and stir to dissolve. Transfer to a bucket, cover and allow to cool. At fermentation temperature, add the pectic enzyme, acid, tannin and yeast starter and stir well. Cover and leave to ferment for 5 days, keeping well covered and stirring twice daily. Strain into a demijohn and add the remainder of the sugar dissolved in enough water to bring the volume almost to the gallon (4.5 litres). Fit an air-lock. When the first vigorous ferment has died away, top up to the full volume and ferment out as normal. Rack as necessary (the wine is one which will clear very quickly) and store for six months before use.

Notes

- Rosehip pips impart a bitter flavour to the wine if they are crushed, so be careful not to mash the hips.
- Commercially produced *cans of rosehip purée* are available, and can be used to make a good wine quickly and simply.

ROSEHIP WINE (2)

	British	Metric	USA
Rosehip syrup, 1 bottle	12 fl oz	350 ml	12 fl oz
Sugar	2¼ lb	1 kg	1¾ lb
Citric acid	2 tsp	2 tsp	2 tsp
Liquid malt extract	8 oz	225 g	8 oz
Tannin	⅛ tsp	⅛ tsp	⅛ tsp
Yeast and nutrient			
Water to	1 gallon	4.5 litres	1 gallon

Follow the recipe for Blackcurrant Wine (2), page 118, using rosehip syrup in place of Ribena.

ROSEHIP AND ORANGE WINE

Add 1¾ pints (1 litre) of pure unsweetened orange juice to any of the above recipes, but omit the citric acid. Delicious, cheap and very good.

ROSEHIP AND FIG WINE

A superb wine can be made by adding the "juice" obtained by boiling 1 lb (450 g) of figs or 4 oz (110 g) of dried figs in 2 pints (1.2 litres) of water for 10 minutes to any of the above Rosehip recipes. Alternatively, the figs may be added to the pulp fermentation. In this case, the boiling water should be poured over them before the pulp fermentation begins.

ROSE PETAL WINE

This can be very attractive, with a delicate flavour, colour and bouquet, but the results do vary according to the petals used.

	British	Metric	USA
Fresh rose petals (red, scented)	4 pints	2.3 litres	4 pints

	British	Metric	USA
or Dried petals	3 oz	85 g	3 oz
Concentrated white or rosé grape juice	½ pint	300 ml	½ pint
Sugar	1¾ lb	800 g	1½ lb
Citric acid	1 tsp	1 tsp	1 tsp
Tannin	¼ tsp	¼ tsp	¼ tsp
Yeast and nutrient			
Water to	1 gallon	4.5 litres	1 gallon

Wash the rose petals gently and then soak them in 6 pints (3.5 litres) of water containing a dissolved Campden tablet, for 24 hours. Stir in the grape concentrate, acid and tannin, and add the yeast starter. Ferment on the "pulp" for 5 days before straining into a demijohn and adding the sugar dissolved in enough water to make the volume up to 1 gallon (4.5 litres). Fit an air-lock and ferment out as usual. (The use of rosé grape concentrate will obviously provide more colour than the use of white concentrate. This is really a matter of personal taste.)

SEVILLE ORANGE WINE

	British	Metric	USA
Seville oranges	4 lb	1.8 kg	3½ lb
Sweet oranges	4	4	4
Lemon	1	1	1
Sultanas	1 lb	450 g	1 lb
Sugar	2½ lb	1.15 kg	2 lb
Pectic enzyme			
Yeast and nutrient			
Water to	1 gallon	4.5 litres	1 gallon

Thinly pare the rind from the oranges, avoiding the white pith, which is very bitter. Place the pieces of rind in a basin and heat them in a low oven until they are slightly brown and crisp. This will drive off the oil of orange which can interfere with the fermentation, while leaving enough flavour to produce a good wine. Wash and chop the sultanas and pour 5 pints (2.8 litres) of boiling water over them. Leave to cool, then add the orange rinds, the juice of the oranges and lemon, the pectic enzyme and the sugar dissolved in enough water to bring the volume up to just under the gallon (4.5 litres). At 20°C (68°F), add a yeast starter, stir well and cover. Ferment on pulp for 5 days, keeping well covered and stirring twice daily. Then strain into a demijohn, top up if necessary, fit an air-lock and ferment out. Rack when wine begins to clear and again when perfectly bright.

See also Orange Wine, page 148; Fruit Juice Wines, pages 133-5.

SLOE WINE

	British	Metric	USA
Fresh, ripe sloes	3 lb	1.35 kg	3 lb
or Dried sloes	1 lb	450 g	1 lb
Ripe bananas, peeled	1 lb	450 g	1 lb
or Dried bananas	6 oz	170 g	6 oz
Concentrated red grape juice	9 oz	250 g	⅓ pint
Sugar	2¼ lb	1 kg	1¾ lb
Tartaric acid	1 tsp	1 tsp	1 tsp
Pectic enzyme			
Yeast and nutrient			
Water to	1 gallon	4.5 litres	1 gallon

Wash the sloes and place them in a bucket. Dissolve the sugar in 4 pints (2.3 litres) of boiling water and pour this solution over the fruit. Mash gently. Add the liquid obtained by simmering the peeled, chopped bananas in 2 pints (1.2 litres) of water for 15 minutes. When at 20°–25°C (67°–75°F), add all the other ingredients and make the volume up to 1 gallon (4.5 litres) with cooled, boiled water. Ferment on pulp for 4 days, keeping well covered and stirring twice daily, before straining into a demijohn. Top up if necessary, fit an air-lock and ferment to dryness.

SLOE, BLACKBERRY AND ELDERBERRY

(By Mr A.F. Hendrie, of Keswick, Cumbria)

	British	Metric	USA
Sloes	3 lb	1.35 kg	2½ lb
Blackberries	1 lb	450 g	1 lb
Dates (compressed type, cut thinly)	4 oz	110 g	4 oz
Juice of ½ lb (225 g) of elderberries			
Sugar	2lb 10 oz	1.2 kg	2¼ lb
Acid	As required		
Yeast and nutrient			
Water to	1 gallon	4.5 litres	1 gallon

Pour boiling water over fruit and dates in bucket. Crush, stir and allow to cool. Add 1 Campden tablet and 24 hours later the nutrient, acid, yeast and half the sugar in solution. Leave for 4 days, stirring occasionally, then strain into demijohn and add remaining sugar in solution. Should ferment out dry in five weeks or so. Finally, add one more Campden tablet and leave in a cool place for at least a month. Rack off and bottle. The wine should be quite clear, although I usually filter to obtain a polished appearance. Drink this "Bordeaux" after a year.

SULTANA WINE (1)

	British	Metric	USA
Sultanas, washed, drained and chopped*	2 lb	900 g	1¾ lb
Sugar	2 lb	900 g	1¾ lb
Citric acid	2 tsp	2 tsp	2 tsp
Pectic enzyme			
Yeast and nutrient			
Water to	1 gallon	4.5 litres	1 gallon

(*The sultanas may be chopped, or squashed in the fermentation bin after they have swollen.) Place the fruit in the bin or bucket and pour 7 pints (4 litres) of boiling water in which the sugar has been dissolved over it. Cover and leave to cool, then add the yeast and other ingredients. Stir well. Ferment on the pulp for 7 days, keeping well covered and stirring twice daily. Then strain into a demijohn and press the fruit pulp gently to extract the maximum liquid. If much pulp passes through the strainer, pass the liquid again through a fine mesh strainer (not a filter!). Top up to the gallon (4.5 litres), fit an air-lock and ferment to dryness. A wine of surprising quality, ready after six months. The addition of 1 pint (550 ml) of fruit juice (reduce the water accordingly) can provide many "variations on a theme".

SULTANA WINE (2)

(Courtesy of Bath Wine Circle)

	British	Metric	USA
Sultanas	1 lb	450 g	1 lb
Banana	1	1	1
Rice	3 oz	85 g	3 oz
Sugar	2½ lb	1.15 kg	2 lb
Acid	1½ tsp	1½ tsp	1½ tsp
Yeast and nutrient			
Water to	1 gallon	4.5 litres	1 gallon

Bring 1 gallon (4.5 litres) of water to the boil and dissolve the sugar while boiling. Place sultanas and chopped banana in plastic bucket and pour on the sugar solution. Bring 6 oz (170 g) of water to the boil and add the rice, bring back to boil, and boil for 3 minutes. Strain this liquid onto the sultanas, allow to cool and then add all other ingredients and yeast starter. Allow to ferment for 5 days then strain into gallon (4.5 litres) jar and fit air-lock. This wine can be used as a base for any type of fruit white wine. Even though simple, it does produce a wine of surprising quality.

TEA WINE

Some of the pure, delicately scented blends of tea make unusual and attractive wines. However, to my mind there is little to be gained from making wine from ordinary cheap household tea.

	British	Metric	USA
Tea	12 tsp	12 tsp	12 tsp
Concentrated white grape juice	¾ pint	425 ml	¾ pint
Sugar	1¾ lb	800 g	1½ lb
Citric acid	1 tsp	1 tsp	1 tsp
Yeast and nutrient			
Pectic enzyme			
Water to	1 gallon	4.5 litres	1 gallon

Make up a must with the grape concentrate and 4 pints (2.3 litres) of water. Add the other ingredients and a yeast starter. Mix well and transfer to a small fermenting jar with no air-space. Cover the neck of the jar but ensure that the gas produced by fermentation can escape. Leave until the first violent ferment has ended. When this has happened, infuse the tea in 2 pints (1.2 litres) of boiling water, stir in the sugar and leave for 10 minutes. Then strain the tea into a demijohn and allow to cool before adding the prepared must. Mix well and top up to 1 gallon (4.5 litres) if necessary. Fit an air-lock and ferment out. Needs little if any maturation. The idea of preparing the wine in the way described above is to prevent the gas from driving off the scent of the tea.

WHEAT WINE

	British	Metric	USA
Wheat (grain)	2 lb	900 g	1¾ lb
Sultanas	1 lb	450 g	12 oz
Sugar	2¼ lb	900 g	1¾ lb
Citric acid	1 tsp	1 tsp	1 tsp

| Grape tannin | ½ tsp | ½ tsp | ½ tsp |

Grape tannin   ½ tsp   ½ tsp   ½ tsp
Fungal amylase or diastase
Pectic enzyme (if using sultanas)
Yeast and nutrient
Water to   1 gallon   4.5 litres   1 gallon

Method as for Barley Wine, pages 112.

WHITECURRANT WINE

As for Redcurrant Wine, page 159, but use white grape concentrate rather than red.

WHINBERRY OR WHORTLEBERRY

See Bilberry Wine, pages 114-16.

WHITE TABLE WINE

Apples make a useful general purpose white wine which can be prepared in quantity in several ways, for example:

1. Use a fruit crusher to mash the apples, place the pulp in linen bags and press to extract the juice. Dilute in proportion one-third apple juice to two-thirds water (or according to taste), then dissolve 2 Campden tablets per gallon (4.5 litres) and leave for 24 hours. Next, measure the S.G. and add sugar as required — usually about 3 lb (1.35 kg) for each gallon (4.5 litres) of liquid — transfer to carboy, cask or demijohns, add a yeast starter and leave it to ferment. (3 lb/1.35 kg sugar added to 1 gallon/4.5 litres is equivalent to 2½ lb/1.15 kg sugar dissolved in liquid to give a *total* volume of one gallon 4.5 litres.)

2. Chop or mash the apples, add sulphited water (2 Campden tablets per gallon/4.5 litres) and Rohament P enzyme to purée the fruit; leave for 24 hours. Then add a yeast starter, ferment for 7 days before straining off the pulp. Stir in sugar as required and transfer to cask, carboy or demijohns for fermentation.

- For winemakers without ready access to large quantities of apples, a good standby for white wine is fruit juice. The quantity of juice is not critical, neither is the mix. Here is one suggested recipe for 5 gallons (22.5 litres); the quantities are pro rata for smaller volumes:

	British	Metric	USA
Concentrated white grape juice	2½ pints	1.5 litres	2½ pints
Pure orange juice	4 pints	2.3 litres	4 pints
Pure grapefruit juice	4 pints	2.3 litres	4 pints
Sugar	See text		
Tannin	1 tsp	1 tsp	1 tsp
Yeast and nutrient			
Water to	5 gallons	22.5 litres	5 gallons

Mix the juices together with 21 pints (11.9 litres) of boiled water to produce 4 gallons (18 litres) of must. Measure the S.G. and calculate the amount of sugar present in the juices, remembering that the figures in the table on page 60 should be multiplied by 4 to take account of the total volume. The total weight of sugar needed will be 11½ lb (5.2 kg). Determine how much sugar is required and add it as syrup, dissolved in enough water to bring the total volume up to 5 gallons (22.5 litres). Add the tannin, introduce a vigorous yeast starter and transfer to fermentation vessels under air-lock. Proceed as normal; the wine will be ready to drink soon after the second racking.

PART 3

Making "Sherry" and Sparkling Wines

MAKING SHERRY

Once you have acquired the basic winemaking skills, you may wish to try something more sophisticated. The ideal place to start is with a home-made "sherry". Of course it is not possible to build at home the complicated solera system of casks which is responsible for the consistently high quality of commercial sherries, but a reasonable imitation can be produced if some care is exercised.

The flavour characteristic of pale dry (fino and amontillado) sherries is derived from the oxidation of the wine (page 81), in conjunction with the growth of a certain special type of yeast called a *flor* on the surface of the wine after normal fermentation is complete. Obtaining this growth can be tricky for the home-winemaker. The balance of the original must needs to be correct, which is one reason why gypsum is added (the other being that it helps to develop the flavour). However, if the flor does not grow, the wine can be sweetened and served as a sweet or "cream" sherry, in which flor never develops, but which is still exposed to the air to produce the oxidation.

DRY APPLE SHERRY

	British	Metric	USA
Pure apple juice	1¾ pints	1 litre	1¾ pints
Sherry type grape concentrate	1 pint	550 ml	1 pint
Sugar	1½ lb	680 g	1¼ lb
Gypsum (Calcium sulphate)	1 oz	30 g	1 oz
Tartaric acid	½ tsp	½ tsp	½ tsp
Grape tannin	½ tsp	½ tsp	½ tsp
Sherry flor yeast and nutrient			

Mix the fruit juice and concentrate with half the sugar and enough water to produce a total volume of 6½ pints (3.7 litres). Add the gypsum, acid, tannin and a vigorous sherry flor yeast starter of not more than ¾ pint (425 ml) volume. Transfer to a demijohn and fit an air-lock. Ferment for three weeks or until the S.G. reaches 1.003, then dissolve extra sugar in the wine in 4-oz (110 g) lots until a dry wine of high alcoholic strength is achieved. Note: To ensure that the sherry will be dry, do not allow the S.G. to exceed 1.003 at any time during the addition of sugar.

When the fermentation has finished, rack the wine carefully into a second demijohn. This should be only seven-eighths full. Do not add any Campden tablets! Replace the bung and air-lock with a sterile cotton-wool plug. Set the wine aside in a cool (15°–17°C/59°–62°F), dry place and leave totally undisturbed. The formation of a flor may take weeks or months; it appears as a thin, greyish film on the surface of the wine. Leave the wine undisturbed until the flor has completely distintegrated and formed a sediment on the bottom. The sherry may then be bottled. If no flor has formed after six months, stabilize the wine, add sugar to taste and bottle. It will still have a sherry-like flavour. The wine is best stored for about nine months before use and will certainly improve with keeping.

OTHER RECIPES

Suitable ingredients include yellow plums, peaches, rosehips, sultanas and so on. Red fruits are not suitable. The must is prepared in the normal way and pulp fermented. For example:

DRY APRICOT SHERRY

	British	Metric	USA
Fresh apricots	3 lb	1.35 kg	2½ lb
or Dried apricots	1 lb	450 g	1 lb
Sultanas	8 oz	225 g	8 oz
or Concentrated white grape juice	½ pint	300 ml	½ pint

Sugar	2¾ lb	1.25 kg	2¼ lb
Tartaric acid	2 tsp	2 tsp	2 tsp
Gypsum (calcium sulphate)	1 oz	30 g	1 oz
Grape tannin	½ tsp	½ tsp	½ tsp
Pectic enzyme			
Sherry flor yeast and nutrient			
Water to	1 gallon	4.5 litres	1 gallon

Chop and boil any dried fruit before use. Then mix the fruit and liquid with any fresh fruit and the concentrate in a fermentation bin. Add half the sugar as syrup and all the other ingredients before making up to a total volume of about 7 pints (4 litres). Ensure the temperature is not above 25°C (75°F) introduce the yeast starter. Stir well and ferment on pulp for 5 days, keeping well covered and stirring twice daily. Then strain into a demi-john, topping up slightly if necessary. Fit an air-lock and proceed as for Apple Sherry (above).

SWEET SHERRY

As explained above, the flavour of sweet sherry originates from the oxidation in the later stages of storage under a porous cotton-wool plug. A sherry flor cannot form, so there is no point using a flor yeast; a normal sherry or port yeast will be satisfactory. The recipe below is for "Cream Sherry" and was devised by the late Mr Charles Hewett. It is reproduced by courtesy of Mrs Grace Parsons of "Hayes Home Brew".

	British	*Metric*	*USA*
Sugar	3½ lb	1.6 kg	3 lb
Crystal malt	1 lb	450 g	1 lb
Chopped raisins	1 lb	450 g	1 lb
Citric acid	½ tsp	½ tsp	½ tsp
Grape tannin	½ tsp	½ tsp	½ tsp
Pectolase			
Port or Sherry yeast and nutrient			

Coarsely chop the raisins. Using a bucket with a lid mix the crystal malt, 2 lb (900 g) of sugar and raisins. Pour on 2½ pints (1.5 litres) of boiling water to dissolve the sugar and leave for ½ hour. Then add 5 pints (2.8 litres) of cold water, add the other ingredients and leave for 24 hours, keeping well covered. Prepare the yeast according to instructions on the packet and add to the must. When the fermentation has begun keep in a warm place at a temperature of between 20° – 25°C (68° – 78°F) and stir daily. On the seventh day dissolve the remaining sugar in 1 pint (600 ml) of boiling water, when cool add to the must and leave for 2 days. Strain through a nylon sieve into a glass fermentation jar. Fill the jar to the bottom of the neck with cold water and continue fermentation under an air-lock for about 4 weeks. Rack off into a clean jar, replace the air-lock with a bung of cotton wool and leave until clear. Rack off and bottle.

Notes

- Specific gravity should be 1020 or lower.
- Sweeten with sugar syrup 1020–1035.
- Fortify each bottle with a sherry glass of cheap brandy.
- To make a medium-sweet sherry use 4 oz less sugar at second stage and take down to 1005–1010 S.G.

MAKING SPARKLING WINE

Sparkling wine is not difficult to make at home, and is well worth the time and effort involved. The procedure involves two stages: firstly, a normal fermentation to produce a wine of no more than 10% alcohol by volume; and secondly, another fermentation in the bottle to produce the bubbles of carbon dioxide gas which give the wine its sparkle.

To avoid the danger of bottles exploding during the second stage, you should follow the instructions below carefully.

The most important points to remember are:

1.   A comparatively low alcohol level (8%–10%) from the first stage of fermentation is necessary because the Champagne yeast used in the bottle fermentation cannot tolerate much higher levels.

2.   It is necessary to use a Champagne yeast during the bottle fermentation because it is the only yeast able to work under high gas pressure and because it will not taint the wine.

3.   The high gas pressures generated during bottle fermentation make it absolutely essential to use only Champagne bottles, which have extra thick glass. They can be obtained from home winemaking shops or restaurants. Ordinary bottles will burst.

The first stage

A suitable must is prepared in the normal way. This should be one which will give a light, well-flavoured wine — orange, apple, yellow plum, sultana, gooseberry or Champagne grape concentrate are all suitable. The sugar content of this must should not exceed 1 lb 14 oz per gallon (which equals 850 grams per 4.5 litres, and 1 lb 9 oz per US gallon) or the level of alcohol may be too high to permit the bottle fermentation. An initial S.G. of about S.G. 1.075 or less will be about right. The wine is fermented to dryness and left to clear. An S.G. of 1.000 or less is absolutely essential. Remember that chemical stabilizers or preservatives such as Campden tablets must not be added because they will inhibit the bottle fermentation.

The second stage

First of all, a small amount of sugar is dissolved in the new wine. This provides the sugar for the bottle fermentation. The optimum amount is 2½ oz (70 g) per gallon (4.5 litres) and *on no account must this be exceeded or the bottles may explode.*

Next, a culture of dried Champagne yeast is reactivated in ⅕ pint (100 ml) of water containing only a pinch of sugar. After six hours, an equal volume of wine is mixed in; and after a further six hours more wine is added to double the volume once again. The volume is doubled up in this way until the yeast is active in the full volume of the wine. (The ferment will *not* be very vigorous.) Be sure to take all hygienic precautions and do not leave any wine open to the air.

Fig 7: Making sparkling wines

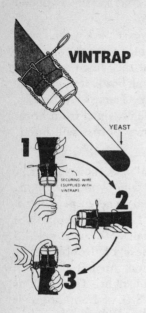

VINTRAP

YEAST

SECURING WIRE
(SUPPLIED WITH
VINTRAP)

Left: The Southern Vinyards *Vintrap*, ideal for making sparkling wine. Diagrams 1–3 illustrate the way in which the plastic tube is tied down to the bottle before opening.

Below: Two alternative methods of storing wine bottles with Vintraps attached. Southern Vinyards will be able to supply details. Another alternative would be to use a standard cardboard wine bottle case with holes cut in the bottom so the Vintraps could protrude through. The box would be supported on bricks at a suitable angle.

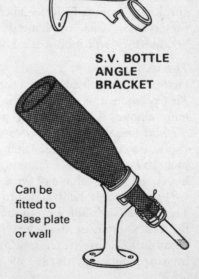

S.V. BOTTLE ANGLE BRACKET

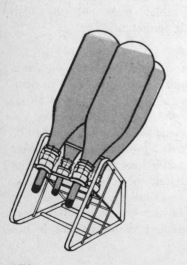

Can be fitted to Base plate or wall

When the whole bulk of the wine is fermenting, siphon it into sterile, but well rinsed, champagne bottles. Leave an air-space of two inches (50 mm) over the wine. There are at this stage two alternative procedures. The first is to use the Southern Vinyards *Vintrap* stopper, the purpose of which is described below; the second is to use conventional white plastic dome-shaped stoppers. In either case, the stoppers must fit into the bottle neck very tightly and be tied down with the wire loop or *muselet* supplied.

For the first week after this has been done, the bottles should be stored at room temperature to allow the bottle fermentation to begin. They can then be moved to a cooler place (15°C/60°F) for longer storage and maturation.

During this period of storage and maturation, Champagne bottles are moved gradually from a horizontal to an upside-down position so that the yeast slides down into the stopper. The Vintrap, in fact, has a small plastic tube or blister protruding from the stopper and the yeast falls into this. Ordinary stoppers arc hollow and the yeast collects in the dome. To encourage the yeast sedimentation, the bottles must be given a sharp twist every two days or so for one month before use. (Do not shake the bottles.)

When the wine is ready to serve, the yeast deposit is first removed from the bottle. And this is where the Vintrap comes into its own, for the plastic tube is simply tied down to the side of the bottle: the bottle is then chilled, and the wine can be opened and served at once. Figure 7 (opposite) illustrates this in detail.

With an ordinary stopper, however, the procedure is not as simple. The approach usually recommended is to chill the wine to 10°C (50°F) and then insert the lowest part of the bottleneck into a freezing mixture of equal parts of salt and crushed ice. A block of ice will form in the neck or stopper and encapsulate the sediment. (The wine bottle should be wrapped in a towel to stop it warming up during the time required for the freezing to take place.) The muselet is then untied, the stopper removed and the pellet of frozen wine containing the yeast allowed to shoot out of the bottle. As soon as this has happened, another stopper is banged in and tied down. The wine can then be stored and

179

served in the normal way. Obviously this is a somewhat tricky procedure and I recommend the use of the Vintrap.

If you want to produce a medium dry or sweet sparkling wine, the best method is to add the non-fermentable sugar lactose to taste at the beginning of the bottle fermentation.

GOOSEBERRY "CHAMPAGNE"

	British	Metric	USA
Hard green gooseberries	3½ lb	1.55 kg	3 lb
Concentrated white grape juice	9 oz	250 g	⅓ pint
Sugar	1 lb 10 oz	725 g	1 lb 5oz
Citric acid	1½ tsp	1½ tsp	1½ tsp
Pectic enzyme			
Yeast and nutrient			
Water to	1 gallon	4.5 litres	1 gallon

Top and tail the gooseberries. Place them in a fermentation bin and pour on 4 pints (2.3 litres) of boiling water. Mash well, cover and leave to cool. At 20°–25°C (68°–75°F), add the concentrate, acid, enzyme and a yeast starter, together with the sugar dissolved in enough water to bring the volume up to 1 gallon (4.5 litres). Ferment on pulp for 4 days, keeping well covered and stirring twice daily. Strain into a demijohn, top up if necessary, fit an air-lock and ferment to dryness. Rack as necessary and allow to clear.

If a medium-dry or medium-sweet champagne is required, dissolve lactose to your taste in the wine. Then add 2½ oz (70 g) of sucrose and a Champagne yeast as described on page 177. Siphon into Champagne bottles, fit plastic stoppers and leave to mature. Chill to about 10°C (50°F) before serving.

ELDERFLOWER "CHAMPAGNE"

	British	Metric	USA
Elderflowers (lightly pressed down)	1 pint	550 ml	1 pint
or Dried elderflowers	1 oz	30 g	1 oz
Concentrated white grape juice	½ pint	300 ml	½ pint
Sugar	1 lb 10 oz	725 g	1 lb 5 oz
Citric acid	2 tsp	2 tsp	2 tsp
Grape tannin	⅛ tsp	⅛ tsp	⅛ tsp
Yeast and nutrient			
Water to	1 gallon	4.5 litres	1 gallon

Pick the flowers on a dry day. Comb them gently off the stalks and place them in 5 pints of water (2.8 litres) containing a dissolved Campden tablet. Cover and leave for 24 hours. Then dissolve the sugar in 1 pint (550 ml) of water and add the solution to the flowers, together with the concentrate, acid and tannin. Check that the must is at fermentation temperature, and add the yeast starter. Mix well, cover, and leave to ferment on pulp for 3 days, keeping well covered and stirring twice daily. Strain off into a demijohn, top up if necessary and fit an air-lock. Ferment out in the normal way. Rack the wine and proceed as for Gooseberry Champagne, page 180.

APPENDIX I

Measurement Conversion Information

TO CONVERT FROM   TO

Pounds	Kilograms	Multiply by 0.45
Kilograms	Pounds	Multiply by 2.2
Ounces	Grams	Multiply by 28
Grams	Ounces	Multiply by 0.035
Fl oz (British)	Millilitres	Multiply by 28.4
Ml	Fl oz	Multiply by 0.035
Pints (British)	Litres	Multiply by 0.57
Litres	Pints	Multiply by 1.75
Gallons (British)	Litres	Multiply by 4.55
Litres	Gallons	Multiply by 0.22
Fahrenheit	Centigrade	Subtract 32 then Multiply by 0.55
Centigrade	Fahrenheit	Multiply by 1.8 then add 32

APPENDIX II

Hydrometer Chart
for American Readers

This chart takes account of the smaller volume of the United States gallon, and should not be confused with the chart giving British and Metric measurements on page 60.

Specific Gravity	Amount of sugar in 1 US gallon lb	oz	Potential alcohol (% by volume)
1.010		4	1.4
1.015		6	2.0
1.020		8	2.8
1.025		9	3.4
1.030		11	4.1
1.035		13	4.8
1.040		15	5.5
1.045	1	0	6.2
1.050	1	2	6.9
1.055	1	4	7.6
1.060	1	6	8.2
1.065	1	7	8.9
1.070	1	9	9.5
1.075	1	10	10.2
1.080	1	12	11.0
1.085	1	14	11.6
1.090	2	0	12.3
1.095	2	2	13.0
1.100	2	4	13.6
1.105	2	5	14.4
1.110	2	7	15.0
1.115	2	9	15.7
1.120	2	11	16.4

APPENDIX III
Glossary of Winemaking Terms

Acetification

The turning of a wine to vinegar by bacterial infection.

Acid

The acids in a wine must provide sharpness and flavour; they also ensure the yeast has an environment suitable for fermentation. There are three main types of acid: citric, the acid of citrus fruits; tartartic, the acid of grapes and other fruits; and malic acid, the acid chiefly of apples.

Aerobic fermentation

The first part of the fermentation, conducted in the presence of air, during which yeast builds up a strong colony of cells.

Air-lock

A glass or plastic device which excludes external air from the fermentation vessel, but allows carbon dioxide to escape.

Anaerobic fermentation

The second part of the fermentation, conducted under air-lock.

Bentonite

A fining agent made of clay particles which swell in water.

Bite

The astringency of a wine, produced by tannin. Without sufficient tannin, a wine may taste flat and insipid.

Body

The body of wine refers to its fullness. The opposite is "thin", which means a wine tastes thin and watery.

Bouquet

The aroma or "nose" of a wine which develops during storage in bulk containers or bottles. Produced by slow chemical reactions between acids and alcohol in the wine.

Campden Tablets

Small tablets of compressed sodium metabisulphite powder which are used to make up sterilizing solution or to protect a wine against oxidation or infection during storage.

Carbon Dioxide

Odourless, harmless gas produced during fermentation by the action of yeast on sugar dissolved in the must.

Clearing

The natural process by which sediment drops out of a wine after fermentation, to form a deposit of lees and leave the wine clear.

Demijohn

Glass jar for fermentation. It has a capacity of just over a gallon (4.5 litres) and fills six standard wine bottles.

Diastase

The enzyme which converts starch to sugar and thus prevents starch haze in a finished wine. Also known as fungal amylase.

Dry

The opposite of sweet. A dry wine has no taste of sweetness, although it may still contain a tiny amount of sugar.

Enzyme

A chemical compound which can effectively convert complex molecules (such as starch) to simpler ones (such as sugar). Enzymes produced by yeast cells convert sugar into alcohol during fermentation.

Esters

The chemical compounds responsible for the bouquet of wine.

Fermentation

The conversion of sugar into alcohol and carbon dioxide under certain conditions by yeast cells. (See also *malo-lactic fermentation*.)

Fermentation lock or trap See *air-lock*.

Filtration

The removal of minute particles suspended in a wine by passing it through a filter medium.

Fining

The clearing of a wine by adding any substance which will coagulate suspended matter and form a sediment.

Finished wine

A wine in which the processes of fermentation and clearing are complete.

Flor

A growth of yeast cells formed on the surface of a wine during the making of sherry.

Fortification

The addition of alcohol to a finished wine to increase its alcoholic strength.

Fructose

A simple sugar, one of the constituents of sucrose.

Glucose

Another simple sugar; the other constituent of sucrose (see *fructose*).

Grape sugar

Glucose and fructose.

Hydrometer

An instrument for estimating the sugar content of a must or finished wine.

Invert sugar

A preparation of glucose and fructose obtained by boiling sucrose solution with some added citric acid. Yeast can ferment invert sugar, but has to convert sucrose enzymatically to glucose and fructose before fermentation.

Invertase

The enzymes produced by yeast which convert sucrose into glucose and fructose.

Isinglass

A proteinaceous compound used to fine wine.

Lactic acid

An acid produced during the malo-lactic fermentation. Can also be added to a wine must in place of citric, malic or tartaric acid; it helps develop a good bouquet.

Lees

See *sediment*.

Malo-lactic fermentation

A reaction caused by the lactic acid bacterium converting malic acid into lactic acid in a wine where the normal fermentation is complete. Can be avoided by careful hygiene and sterilization.

Maturation

The change in wine which takes place during storage. It involves subtle chemical changes that produce a good bouquet and the precipitation of excess tannin (in red wines) to form a sediment. The flavour of a wine mellows during its maturation.

Metabisulphite

Sodium metabisulphite powder. It dissolves in water to form a potent sterilizing agent, sulphur dioxide gas.

Nutrients

Chemical compounds (ammonium sulphate, phosphate and vitamin B) which encourage the growth of yeast.

Oxidation

A process whereby alcohol is converted to aldehyde compounds, thus spoiling a wine's flavour, colour and bouquet. However, carefully controlled oxidation can be used to produce sherry.

Pectic enzyme

An enzyme needed to break down pectin, a gummy carbohydrate substance found in fruit which may cause haziness in a finished wine.

Primary fermentation

See *aerobic fermentation.*

Pulp fermentation

Any fermentation conducted in the presence of the pulped fruit or other ingredients.

Racking

A process of siphoning a wine off the sediment formed after fermentation.

Secondary fermentation

See *anaerobic fermentation.*

Sediment

The deposit formed at the bottom of the fermentation vessel when fermentation is complete. It is composed of dead or dormant yeast cells, fruit sediment, and so on.

Sucrose

The chemical name for ordinary household sugar. It is composed of glucose and fructose molecules combined to form a complex sugar.

Sulphur dioxide

The gas produced by dissolving sodium metabisulphite powder in water. It acts as a sterilizing agent.

Tannin

An astringent substance which is found in the skin of red fruits. It is an important ingredient of many wines, providing a vital element of the overall flavour.

Vinegar

Acetic acid. This may be formed in a wine if it becomes infected by types of bacteria often carried by the "vinegar fly" or "fruit fly" *Drosophila*.

Yeast

A small, single-celled organism, *Saccharomyces*, which carries out fermentation. Only the true wine yeast can work adequately for the home-winemaker.

Zymase

The enzymes produced by yeast which convert glucose and fructose into alcohol.

INDEX